If you can believe
then all things will be possible

If You Can Believe
© Copyright 2021 by Paul Balius
Published by HA'KODESH PUBLISHING

ISBN 978-1-7349097-5-3 (hardcover)
ISBN 978-1-7349097-2-2 (paperback)
ISBN 978-1-7349097-3-9 (epub)

Editorial services by Thomas Womack, *BookOx.com*

Proofreading by Dana L. Cobb

Design by Monica Thomas for TLC Book Design, *TLCBookDesign.com*

Mountain scene © guvendemir, istockphoto by Getty Images
Dove imagery © nur, Adobe Stock

Unless otherwise indicated, Scripture quotations are from:
The Holy Bible, New King James Version (NKJV) © 1984 by Thomas Nelson, Inc.

Other Scripture quotations are from:

New American Standard Bible® (NASB) © 1960, 1977, 1995 by the Lockman Foundation. Used by permission.

The Amplified Bible (AMP) © 1965, 1987 by Zondervan Publishing House. The Amplified New Testament © 1958, 1987 by the Lockman Foundation.

The Amplified Bible, Classic Edition (AMPC) © 1954, 1958, 1962, 1964, 1965, 1987 by the Lockman Foundation.

Holy Bible, New Living Translation (NLT) © 1996, 2004 by Tyndale Charitable Trust. Used by permission of Tyndale House Publishers. All rights reserved.

Complete Jewish Bible (CJB) Copyright © 1998 by David H. Stern. All rights reserved.

The Passion Translation® (TPT) copyright © 2017, 2018 by Passion & Fire Ministries, Inc. Used by permission. All rights reserved. ThePassionTranslation.com.

The Names of God Bible (NOG) © 2011 by Baker Publishing Group. From God's Word® © 1995 God's Word to the Nations. Used by permission of Baker Publishing Group.

The Holy Bible, English Standard Version (ESV) © 2001 by Crossway Bibles, a division of Good News Publishers. Used by permission. All rights reserved.

The Holy Bible, New International Version (NIV) © 1973, 1978, 1984, 2011 by Biblica, Inc.™ Used by permission. All rights reserved worldwide.

Contemporary English Version (CEV) © 1995 by American Bible Society

The Living Bible (TLB) © 1971. Used by permission of Tyndale House Publishers, Inc. All rights reserved.

The Holy Bible, King James Version (KJV)

PRINTED IN THE UNITED STATES OF AMERICA

If you can believe

then all things will be possible

PAUL BALIUS

HA'KODESH PUBLISHING

Contents

Bonnie's Prayer vi

Introduction: If You Can Believe ix

1. Word of God 1
2. Your Calling 9
3. Praying for a Miracle 17
4. Trust Me 25
5. Effective Prayers 33
6. A Step of Faith 41
7. Purposes of God 49
8. Saving Figaro 57
9. Saved by God 65
10. Classroom of Adversity 73
11. God's Provisions 83

12. Pray the Promise 91

13. Holy Spirit 99

14. Keep the Faith 107

15. Faith over Fear 115

16. A Faith That Heals 123

17. Spirit Led 131

18. The Lion and the Donkey 139

19. Faith Waits 149

20. Breath of the Spirit 159

21. Raising Amelia 169

22. Pray Like You Mean It 177

23. Plans of God 185

24. All Things are Possible 193

Acknowledgments 202

About the Author 203

Bonnie's prayer

Lord God, in the name of our Lord Jesus Christ, may Your anointing drip down from heaven on the pages of this book as the Holy Spirit moves to impart the Word of Truth to each heart.

I ask for the Light of the Word to illumine this book, so that many people will reach out to grasp it.

I ask for the readers to have a supernatural experience of Your love for them and Your grace over their lives as they read, meditate, and absorb Your words of truth.

I pray that the readers will have the answers to their requests so that many miracles will occur as they believe.

I ask for Your angels to assist in carrying this book to those who want to grow in faith and to all who are in need of Your miraculous help.

Lord, I ask that You will receive honor, reverence, love, and joy from the outcome of this work: If you can believe—then all things will be possible.

—Bonnie Calkins

Bonnie's prayer for the reader to pray

Lord Jesus,

I'm calling out to You.

I approach Your throne of grace with confidence and without fear, because I need Your mercy and grace, to help me in my time of need and I know Your help will come at just the right moment.

Jesus, You said, "if you can believe, all things are possible to him who believes." Therefore, as I bring this request before Your throne, I ask for help to believe so that I might receive a great miracle from Your heart of lovingkindness and mercy.

I ask that as I read the pages of this book Your Holy Spirit will comfort me, instruct me, and increase my faith to believe.

I trust You fully, knowing that You are causing all things to work together for my good even though my mind does not always comprehend what You are doing.

I wait in confidence for Your help!

Amen

INTRODUCTION

If You Can Believe

To the degree that you can believe, things will become possible.

"Jesus said to him, 'If you can believe, all things are possible to him who believes'" (Mark 9:23).

When you see the word *if* in the Bible, you're presented with a choice. You can choose either *yes* or you can choose *no*, but rarely anything in between. If you can believe, then all things are possible. If you can't believe, then not all things are possible. This is not because your faith limits what the Lord can do, but because your faith will limit what the Lord chooses to do. So the things that are possible are up to you—"if you can believe."

The problem we have with believing is that we think we're simply too ill-equipped to believe. We think we need more strength or willpower so that we could do it. But when Jesus said, "If you can believe," He wasn't questioning your abilities, but your willingness. *Growing in faith is not like climbing a mountain, but like falling backward into a deep canyon. One is by your effort; the other has to rely entirely on Him.*

I don't know where you are in your faith right now, but I know God has so much more in store for you. When a person thinks they've reached the end, that's where they'll stop. Don't stop. Your faith has no ending to where it can get to. You can't reach the end of your faith, because your faith is in the One who has no ending. *Your faith journey should be a progression of believing more and doubting less.*

It's easy to think we have a high faith until we're placed in an impossible situation where faith is our only option. It takes an impossible situation to know if we truly think that all things are possible with God.

I don't know if you have a faith that truly believes all things are possible. I don't know how strongly you believe in all that the Lord can do. But what I do know is that no matter how high your faith is, it's far below everything our heavenly Father can do. You can believe more. The Word of God says, "For with God nothing [is or ever] shall be impossible" (Luke 1:37 AMP).

We think that if we first received something, we would then believe more. But there's no faith in that equation. It's the Lord's desire and plan that you should grow in your faith. And to have more faith, you must believe before you receive, not the other way around. If you receive first, then no faith is required, and no faith will be formed. But if you believe first, then your faith will open the way for the receiving. It's in this process that your faith grows and forms ever stronger within you.

The principle is this: *You must believe to receive.*

The more believing, the more receiving—there's no other way. "If you believe, you will receive" (Matthew 21:22 NIV).

When I first became a believer, I didn't believe very much. I gravitated toward an intellectual faith where I could study and prove those things I would then believe in. The more I learned, the more I believed. This level of believing requires little faith. The limit of an intellectual faith is a person's intellect.

It's no wonder so many Christians have so little faith—it's limited by their own capacity, and not unleashed with the unlimited power of God. We need our intellect to learn more, but we need faith to take us higher.

For many years I was blessed to serve in prison ministry. One day in a prison, I was speaking to an inmate who I knew was anointed of God and walking in spiritual gifts. I wanted to live an anointed life, but I didn't know how to get there. So I asked him, "How is it that you're walking in this anointed life?" I'll never forget his answer to me that day. He told me, "I just believed." It's the simplest truths of heaven that confound the wisest of men and women here on earth.

There came a day in my faith journey when I crossed over that bridge—from what I could explain to what I simply believed. I started to read the Word and to believe in all it was saying. I started to take God at His Word. I believed that God could do the impossible, and I started praying with the confidence in all that He can do.

Child of God, there's so much more for you if you will just believe. *Belief is not a finish line, but a journey.*

You can cross this bridge from unbelief to belief. What it takes is not your strength but your surrender. The secret of believing is to just believe. You'll someday kick yourself in the behind for thinking it had to be so much harder than this. Your greatest obstacle to believing is you. Your clever mind tries to make it far more complicated than it really is. You can't strive to gain a thing when it can only be received. Just pray for it. Ask for faith.

As a child of God, simply ask your Father. *Faith is not a prize, but a gift. You can't earn faith; you can only receive it.*

Wherever you are with your faith, it's from there your journey can progress further. Even if you believe little in all that God can do, that's still something. There's not a great distance you must travel in order to believe much; you need to make only a small turn. To believe more, it doesn't take a great effort; it takes a great resting in believing apart from your effort. Most of us are far more adept at coming up with a reason to doubt our heavenly Father than we are at simply believing Him. *Some people spend a lifetime striving to become what God can do for them in a day.*

Child of God, you can grow in your faith. You can have a mountain-moving faith that changes your life and changes the lives of those around you. You can have a faith that stirs the heart of the Father and gains you favor in the throne room of heaven. You don't have to be strong or brilliant to gain this faith, but only be like a child who just believes everything their Father tells them. If our Father says a thing, it is so.

Don't be such a grown-up that you don't simply believe like a child of God. Jesus taught, "Whoever will humble himself therefore and become like this little child [trusting, lowly, loving, forgiving] is greatest in the kingdom of heaven" (Matthew 18:4 AMPC).

Some people have been Christians for years, and yet they believe very little about the power of God. Others have only recently become Christians, and they believe a thing as soon as they read it in the Word. Having a greater faith is accomplished not over long periods of time, but in the moment you're willing to believe.

The hardest ones to convince are usually the smartest ones. Some of the brightest Christians on this planet can argue the power of God right out of their faith, and they think themselves wise in the process. It doesn't take a big mind to have faith, but a surrendered heart. *Until you believe, it's only a theory to you.*

I was a hard case for the Lord Jesus, because I believed in science more than the supernatural. What made it harder for me was that many who taught me in the early years preached more to the mind than to the spirit. We're often led by intellectual arguments and we consider ourselves quite clever for understanding them. But when the spirit of a man or a woman is moved by a supernatural God, there's no longer any place for them to remain clever. It's in that state that a person can be moved to a faith that no longer revolves only around what they can understand.

When I started to grow in my faith and to believe that all things are possible, I was shocked by all that started to happen around me. I looked back at the years in my faith journey where I thought I had faith, but it was such a weak faith. It was a faith that couldn't move a grain of sand, let alone a mountain. But when my faith grew, it grew supernaturally, and I gave up my arguments and gave in to His power.

Dare to step into a life of faith you can't explain.

It's not what you know—it's what you believe. Jesus promised us, "I tell you the truth, if you had faith even as small as a mustard seed, you could say to this mountain, 'Move from here to there,' and it would move. Nothing would be impossible" (Matthew 17:20 NLT).

As I continued to grow in my faith, I started to hear more from the Holy Spirit—in this book I put those words in italics. Only the Word of God is infallible; the rest of us are not. So be discerning with whatever you read from me or anyone else. Use the Word of God as your plumbline, and pray that the Holy Spirit will help you understand the Word even more. In this book I use various Bible versions. Look up these verses in the Bible version you prefer. The best version is the one you read. An even better version is the one you live.

The chapters in this book are from experiences in my faith journey that happened over a span of twenty-one years. All the chapters are in chronological order, and portray the stepping-stones of my faith that the Lord arranged for me along the way. Early on in my faith, I didn't believe nearly as much as I do now. The Lord has used many circumstances to teach me and to build me in my faith.

Consider the stepping-stones in your own faith journey and all that God is teaching you. We're meant to walk in a higher faith—so don't settle for anything less.

You won't get the higher faith until you won't settle for anything less. We have too many settled Christians. "Not that I have already attained, or am already perfected; but I press on, that I may lay hold of that for which Christ Jesus has also laid hold of me" (Philippians 3:12).

Child of God, be determined to believe like a believer. Stop doubting things just because you've not seen them. You have such great potential in the kingdom if you will only start to believe with a faith that has no limits. I'm believing for you and all that God wants to do in your life. You have no idea of the possibilities that exist between you and your heavenly Father.

There are people on this planet counting on you to grow in your faith. Be the one. Dare to believe in what God can do.

You have no idea what lies on the other side of "If you would just believe!" Jesus promised: "All things are possible to him who believes" (Mark 9:23).

Blessings to you,
Paul

1

Word of God

There is nothing impossible for God–not even you.

"For with God nothing is ever impossible and no word from God shall be without power or impossible of fulfillment" (Luke 1:37 AMPC).

IF YOU CAN BELIEVE in the power of God's Word, there will be no limit to how much His Word can change you.

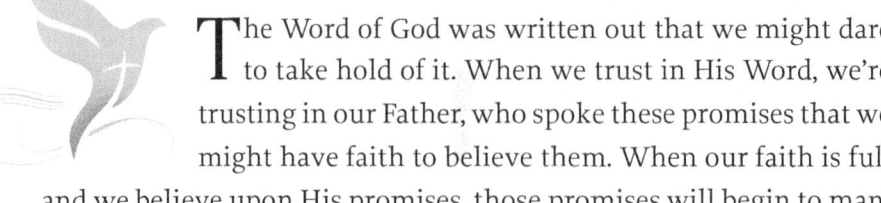

The Word of God was written out that we might dare to take hold of it. When we trust in His Word, we're trusting in our Father, who spoke these promises that we might have faith to believe them. When our faith is full and we believe upon His promises, those promises will begin to manifest in our lives.

Hold God to His Word, and His Word will take hold of you. "He who calls you is faithful, who also will do it" (1 Thessalonians 5:24).

It's one thing to study the Word, and another to be changed by the Word. If we want to grow in our faith, we must grow in our trust in all that the Lord is telling us. To the degree we believe the Word, the Word will change us. The more the Word changes us, the more the power of the Word will flow into us and then through us.

You can hold the Word in your hands, but you can never get your arms around the whole of it. The Lord told the prophet Isaiah, "My word, which comes from my mouth, is like the rain and snow. It will not come back to me without results. It will accomplish whatever I want and achieve whatever I send it to do" (Isaiah 55:11 NOG).

If we think the Word is from man, we'll treat it with caution and concern. But if we acknowledge that the Word is from God, we'll embrace it with awe and adoration. *Our problem is that we treat the Bible more like a novel than the spoken Word of God.* We're better able to argue over its meaning than to be transformed by it.

People seek the myths of man over the truths of God. Myths tell people what they want to hear. God's Word tells them what they need to hear. "One who turns away his ear from hearing the law, even his prayer is an abomination" (Proverbs 28:9).

Learn to acknowledge the Spirit of God in every word that comes off the pages of Holy Scripture. When you read a promise in the Word, stop thinking of it as just a statement of man. When the Lord says a thing, the Lord means it, and you must never doubt Him. There's enough power in the Word of God to change the world, so be assured there's more than enough power in the Word to change you.

No matter how much things are falling apart, God's Word will stand forever. "The grass withers, the flower fades, but the word of our God stands forever" (Isaiah 40:8).

We need to read the Word of God as the promises of God. The Word is not just a history lesson or a mysterious glimpse into the future; it holds the promises of God in what He has for us in this day we live in. Some will try to intellectualize the power out of the Word, and their effort becomes true in their life. But for that man or woman who dares to go on with the Lord in their faith, there's a power and a promise in the Word that God has for them. Don't squander the plans and purposes of God that He has for you by not believing on the truth and power contained in His Word.

It's not enough to know the Word—you must believe the Word. "When you received the word of God which you heard from us, you welcomed it not as the word of men, but as it is in truth, the word of God, which also effectively works in you who believe" (1 Thessalonians 2:13).

I was saved by the power in the Word of God. I'd grown up in the church, but the church hadn't yet been born in me. For the first many years of my life, I ran from the Lord Jesus. One day that all changed. While I was still an unbeliever, I had an unstoppable pressing from the Holy Spirit to buy a Bible, and so I did. I sat down to read it, and not knowing where to begin, I started on page one. And so it began that every day I read the Word of God, along with commentary to help explain it. I kept reading the Word every day until I read it the whole way through.

There's so much power in the Word if we'll only take hold of it! "For the word of God is alive and powerful" (Hebrews 4:12 NLT).

I hadn't made it through the book of Genesis before the Lord Jesus took hold of me. I didn't find Jesus; He found me, and He became real to me through the Word. As I was reading the Word, I saw that the

Word was true and His promises were sure. I didn't understand all I was reading at the time, but I began to experience the faith that comes when you believe in the truth and the power of God's Word.

You can always tell a man or woman immersed in God's Word, because their life will show it. "I rejoice at Your word as one who finds great treasure" (Psalm 119:162).

I've never stopped reading through the Bible since that first time. I just keep reading it over and over again. As I've matured in my faith, the Holy Spirit continues to unravel and reveal deeper truths contained in the Word of God. Every day I find wondrous treasures in the Word. If you approach the Word with the expectation that the Holy Spirit will reveal some precious truth to you, you'll never be disappointed, and you'll be forever growing in your faith.

Though I read the Word of God a thousand times, yet I keep discovering something new each day. "Open my eyes [to spiritual truth] so that I may behold wonderful things from Your law" (Psalm 119:18 AMP).

When I first became a believer, I was all alone with God. By the Lord's design, I've always been a loner. I have a sensory condition that often makes it hard to be outside or around people. When I came to faith, it was in a place of isolation with God. I spent my time in the Word all alone with Him. I used to despise the reasons that made me be alone so much. But over time, I've seen the blessings that have come from it. We can trust God with His plans.

The Word is our foundation to stand on and our peace to take hold of. "Great peace have those who love Your law, and nothing causes them to stumble" (Psalm 119:165).

For years I studied the Word of God and gained knowledge through books and programs. But the majority of my lessons were found in a place of solitude before the Lord while reading His Word. When I read the Word, I believed the Word. I'm convinced that it's from this foundation that my faith has grown.

Friend, it will be in your prayer closet that you'll come to know the Lord the most and be moved by all He can do in your life.

You learn about God in the classroom, but you come to know Him in the prayer closet. "When thou prayest, enter into thy closet, and when thou hast shut thy door, pray to thy Father which is in secret; and thy Father which seeth in secret shall reward thee openly" (Matthew 6:6 KJV).

By the grace of God, I spent several years preaching the Word both in prisons and later on the outside. This was quite the miracle, since I am a loner because of my sensory condition and could barely speak in front of one person, let alone a group. The Lord Jesus can do anything in the life of a believer who believes.

Jesus isn't looking for people who are strong in themselves, but who are weak before Him.

If you want a better life story, you need to put more of God's Word into it. "God's Word is perfect in every way; how it revives our souls! His laws lead us to truth, and His ways change the simple into wise" (Psalm 19:7 TPT).

As I grew in my faith and believed even more, I started to witness a move of God beyond anything I ever could have dreamed. I started to see the Word for what it was, the promises of the Father just waiting for us to believe in them. As I would read the Word, I would live the Word and see its power ever moving.

The promises of God cannot fail.

The world is always trying to change God's Word, but a saint simply lets the Word of God change them. "Forever, O LORD, Your word is settled in heaven [standing firm and unchangeable]" (Psalm 119:89 AMP).

One of the greatest miracles I've seen in my life is what the Lord Jesus did with me. He turned my darkness into His light, and I know He can do the same for you. No matter your situation, Jesus can do wonders in your life. No matter where you are with the Lord Jesus, let Him change you more and more each day. We can't become something new on our own, but only by surrendering to Him and believing upon His ability to change us.

Believe that He can change you. Let Him change you. Stop resisting the Lover of your eternal soul.

Jesus saved you in a moment but will change you over a lifetime. "We can all draw close to him with the veil removed from our faces. And with no veil we all become like mirrors who brightly reflect the glory of the Lord Jesus. We are being transfigured into his very image as we move from one brighter level of glory to another. And this glorious transfiguration comes from the Lord, who is the [Holy] Spirit" (2 Corinthians 3:18 TPT).

The Word of God is the plumb line of truth and the foundation for all our faith. Ever since I got saved, I've stayed in the Word, and the Word has stayed in me. If you want to grow in your faith, you must remain in the Word of God. If you want to understand the depths in the Word of God, it must be revealed to you through the Spirit of God. We can sometimes understand the written words in Scripture, but it takes the Spirit of God to show us the living Word. Pray to the Holy Spirit to open your eyes so that you'll understand and believe upon the truths and the promises found in Holy Scripture.

The Lord can't reveal a new thing until you first have eyes from which you can see—"that the God of our Lord Jesus Christ, the Father of glory, may give you a spirit of wisdom and of revelation in the knowledge of Him. I pray that the eyes of your heart may be enlightened" (Ephesians 1:17-18 NASB).

We'll spend all of eternity searching the truths held within the Word of God, and yet never reach the end. There's more to the Father than the Word has revealed, and there's more in the Word than we've yet to discover.

If you ever think you've reached the end of all that the Word contains—you've only reached the end of what you're willing to see.

Oh, the depths of His Word! We'll never reach the limits of all that's contained in Holy Scripture. "Have you not known? Have you not heard? The everlasting God, the Lord, the Creator of the ends of the earth, neither faints nor is weary. His understanding is unsearchable" (Isaiah 40:28).

It's been a long time since I first believed, yet each day I'm believing even more. *Faith is not still but moving.* Our journey is never over, but should always be reaching for something higher.

You may already be reaching high; keep reaching higher! You may not have reached very high yet, or even doubt that you can. But you can. There's a greater faith you were meant to walk in. And the way to start that is to believe upon the Word of God and its power to change you.

The Word is a light to your soul, so that you'll no longer walk in darkness. "Your word is a lamp to guide my feet and a light for my path" (Psalm 119:105 NLT).

Child of God, my greatest hope is that you'll become immersed in the Word of God every day, and that you'll believe the Word. If you pray to the Holy Spirit to reveal the truths of Scripture to you, and in your heart are willing to receive them, your life will become radically changed for the kingdom and become a blessing to all those around you.

The outcome of your life depends on what you put into it. "Your word I have treasured in my heart, that I may not sin against You" (Psalm 119:11 NASB).

Prayers

✢ *Heavenly Father, show me the truth and the power contained in Your Word, so that Your Word would change me forever.*

✢ *Lord Jesus, help me to understand the Word and the promises contained within. Help me to trust in the depths of the truths and treasures contained in all the Word.*

✳ *Holy Spirit, bring to me, I pray, an ever growing revelation of the depths of God and the riches of His knowledge held within Holy Scripture.*

Spiritual Growth

✳ **Get saved:** You can read in the Word of God that Jesus died for your sins so you can have eternal salvation. If you've accepted His free gift, the words that come from your mouth and the belief you have in your heart will seal what Christ has done for you. Get this right before the Father today. *Turn to the Lord Jesus today, because tomorrow may never come.* "If you confess with your mouth the Lord Jesus and believe in your heart that God has raised Him from the dead, you will be saved" (Romans 10:9).

✳ **Pray Daily:** We get to know the Father by spending time with Him. It's by prayer that we grow closer to the Father, and it's by prayer that the Father draws nearer to us. If you're not praying every day, start doing that today. *More can be accomplished in your morning prayers than in all your efforts throughout the day.* "Don't worry about anything; instead, pray about everything. Tell God what you need, and thank him for all he has done" (Philippians 4:6 NLT).

✳ **Read the Word daily:** You can't live the Word unless you know the Word. If you're not yet reading the Word of God every day, start doing that today. Find a pace that works for you, and never stop doing it. If you don't know where to start, just start at the beginning. *God's Word is the mirror of truth to who you really are.* "All Scripture is inspired by God and is useful to teach us what is true and to make us realize what is wrong in our lives. It corrects us when we are wrong and teaches us to do what is right" (2 Timothy 3:16 NLT).

2

Your Calling

*If God has given you a dream,
He will make a way.*

"Now the Lord spoke to Paul in the night by a vision, 'Do not be afraid, but speak, and do not keep silent; for I am with you, and no one will attack you to hurt you; for I have many people in this city'" (Acts 18:9-10).

IF YOU CAN BELIEVE that the Lord has a calling on your life, you'll be confident in His power to help you achieve it.

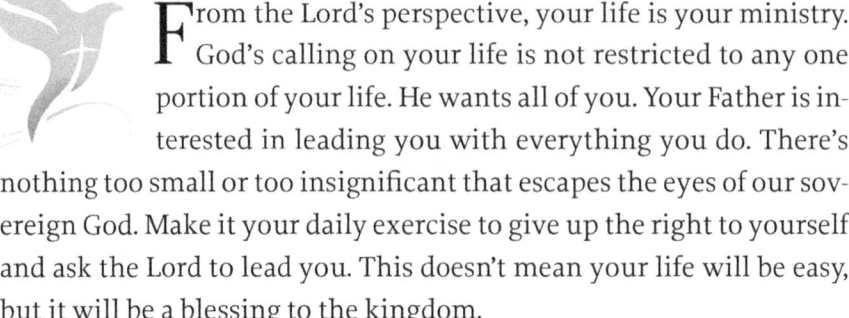

From the Lord's perspective, your life is your ministry. God's calling on your life is not restricted to any one portion of your life. He wants all of you. Your Father is interested in leading you with everything you do. There's nothing too small or too insignificant that escapes the eyes of our sovereign God. Make it your daily exercise to give up the right to yourself and ask the Lord to lead you. This doesn't mean your life will be easy, but it will be a blessing to the kingdom.

Your ministry is to every person who crosses your path. "God has given each of you a gift from his great variety of spiritual gifts. Use them well to serve one another. Do you have the gift of speaking? Then speak as though God Himself were speaking through you. Do you have the gift of helping others? Do it with all the strength and energy that God supplies. Then everything you do will bring glory to God through Jesus Christ" (1 Peter 4:10-11 NLT).

Seek out how the Lord would use you. Press into His calling and be willing to do the little things. It's the little things where we prove our faithfulness to the Lord and where we gain the blessed training of humility. Don't try to pick your ministry, because it's up to God alone what you should do. Your Father knows what's best for you and how you can best serve the kingdom. One of the worst places you can be on this earth is trying to walk in a calling you were never called to walk in. You have to listen to hear your calling.

Your calling is His choice, not yours. "And He Himself gave some to be apostles, some prophets, some evangelists, and some pastors and teachers" (Ephesians 4:11).

When I was very new to my faith, I heard the whisper of the Lord into my heart that I would someday serve Him with writing. I didn't yet understand the Lord's leading, but I believed that the whisper I heard was from Him. At the time, I had no idea of the journey I'd go through, or of the type of writing I'd do. I had the dream placed into my heart, but not yet the instructions of how to get there.

Once He gives you a dream, you must believe that He'll help it to come true.

Nothing is impossible in your dreams, and that's why God will sometimes meet you there. "For God may speak in one way, or in another, yet man does not perceive it. In a dream, in a vision of the night, when deep sleep falls upon men, while slumbering on their beds, then He opens the ears of men, and seals their instruction" (Job 33:14-16).

I'd been traveling weekly to Northern California for my job. Every day at lunch I was listening to a preacher on the radio in my rental car. I went to his church one Sunday, and later I joined his book club. One month the book I received was *Loving God* by Chuck Colson. In one chapter I read about a lady who wrote letters to prisoners. She was in a nursing home, and that was a ministry she could do from there. The very moment I read this chapter, I felt the Lord's leading that this was how I was supposed to start my writing ministry. My first writing assignment from the Lord was to an audience of one.

We need to learn to believe in the leading of the Lord, and then we'll be led by Him.

Even the pagans will answer a call to greatness, but a man or woman of God will answer a call to obscurity. Kingdom success is measured not by how many you reach, but by your obedience in reaching the one you were called to. "Now an angel of the Lord spoke to Philip, saying, 'Arise and go...' So he arose and went" (Acts 8:26-27).

I signed up with Prison Fellowship and began to handwrite letters to an inmate. Then I kept adding more inmates to my list, and eventually I was writing to ten different men spread out across the country, one handwritten letter at a time. I was faithful in this ministry, doing it for seven years. I'm not sure if I moved any of these men with my letters, but in writing the letters, God was moving me.

If you want to change your life, let Him. "Create in me a clean heart, O God, and renew a steadfast spirit within me" (Psalm 51:10).

The Lord can lead you in a hundred different ways, but the question remains: Will you follow Him? Often the leading is in the moment—to that person before you, or to that friend at your side. The leading of the Lord might be to say something, to listen with compassion, or to help them in some practical way. The problem in our day is that people don't want to be led by the Lord; instead they want to be blessed by God in doing whatever they want to do.

God may forgive your disobedience, but He'll bless you in your obedience.

The title you live matters more than the title you have. "As each one has received some spiritual gift, he should use it to serve others" (1 Peter 4:10 CJB).

My sensory condition and difficulty in being around people is one reason I was so glad God asked me to write. Writing was very comfortable for me because I could do it alone. But the Lord has a way about making us uncomfortable, so He can bring about the change He intends to accomplish in us. As I'd felt the leading of the Lord to write to prisoners, I now was feeling the leading of the Lord to do ministry inside prisons. He had me serve inside prisons for the next seven years. After those seven years, He called me out and led me to begin writing for the kingdom in new ways. He spent fourteen years preparing me for the calling I then stepped into.

Don't rush an eternal God whose timing is always perfect.

Apart from divine leading, live within natural lines. He may tell you to walk on water, but until He does, you need to stay in the boat. "And Peter answered Him and said, 'Lord, if it is You, command me to come to You on the water.' So He said, 'Come.'" (Matthew 14:28-29).

What is the Lord calling you to do? Do you believe the Lord can help you reach where He's leading you? You must first believe that He can call you, then be willing to accept whatever He gives you. The calling of the Lord isn't always a single calling for a lifetime; it's often a specific mission for the particular season you're in now. The call of

God is rarely to do something big, but usually something small. Yet it's always a blessing for the kingdom. If you don't believe that the Lord can lead you in small things, don't be surprised if He never leads you into something bigger. Some things you're called to do don't make sense, but if it's from the Lord, just be faithful and do it.

Don't worry about the decisions before you; instead, trust in the leading of the Holy Spirit. "When you turn to the right or turn to the left, you will hear his voice behind you to guide you, saying, 'This is the right path; follow it'" (Isaiah 30:21 TPT).

Sometimes we rush God in our expectation of how long it should take to accomplish His will in our life. For me, it was seven years of writing handwritten letters. Then it was seven more years serving several days each week in various prisons with teaching and preaching. It was only after these fourteen years that the Father finally allowed me to step into the calling that He'd given me so many years before.

The journey is meant to prepare you. The Lord must first entrust you with little before He'll entrust you with more. We cannot graduate to level two until He has first taught us all we need to know on level one.

Don't let imaginary deadlines prevent you from seeking the leading of the Lord. "This is what the LORD says—your Redeemer, the Holy One of Israel: 'I am the LORD your God, who teaches you what is good for you and leads you along the paths you should follow'" (Isaiah 48:17 NLT).

I remember the day and the time when the Lord spoke into my heart that it was time for me to step into the fullness of the writing ministry. It was on a hot July afternoon, and I was outside doing yard work. Why is it that we think God must speak to us at places that make sense to us? I never know when He'll give me a word, but I always trust that anywhere I am, He can give it. On that July afternoon, I heard the Lord say, *"You were meant for something more."* It was not a message to me, but one to be given *through* me. This message was going to be the heartbeat of my writing—I would encourage people that they were meant for something more.

We were not meant for the same, but for more. "And we all, with unveiled face, continually seeing as in a mirror the glory of the Lord, are progressively being transformed into His image from [one degree of] glory to [even more] glory, which comes from the Lord, [who is] the Spirit" (2 Corinthians 3:18 AMP).

Child of God, you were meant for something more. And the something more is found when you come to believe with all your heart in the power and sovereignty of God. When you have Jesus in your heart and the Holy Spirit leading you along the way, your heavenly Father can call out to you and lead you in the way in which you should go. Your Father has a purpose and a plan for your life, and it's up to you to believe upon, listen for, and follow the Lord in everything He would have you do.

Stop looking at the steep mountain you must climb, and just follow the Lord who goes before you. "And the LORD, He is the One who goes before you. He will be with you, He will not leave you nor forsake you; do not fear nor be dismayed" (Deuteronomy 31:8).

Without a vision, there's no plan. Without a plan, there's no purpose. Without a purpose, there's no meaning. *You were meant for something more.* His purposes for you will give you meaning. His plan for you will help you fulfill your purpose. His vision for you will reveal His plans. All you have to do is believe. Nobody crosses a finish line who doesn't start the race. So start. Let the journey of your calling begin today. He'll lead you—just follow Him. He'll give you the vision if only you have eyes to see. I'm praying that you'd follow the dream that He has given you.

Never let go of your dreams. "That night the LORD appeared to Solomon in a dream, and God said, 'What do you want? Ask, and I will give it to you!'" (1 Kings 3:5 NLT).

Prayers

✦ *Heavenly Father, help me to fully realize the truth that You have a plan and a purpose for my life. Help me embrace the truth that You know me, love me, and care about all that I'm doing.*

✦ *Lord Jesus, help me to realize that right now in heaven You're praying for me to become all that You've ordained for me to be.*

✦ *Holy Spirit, guide me, I pray, so that I walk in the plans and the purposes of the Father. Help me see the vision of the purpose the Father has for me.*

Spiritual Growth

✦ **Seek your calling:** God has designed you specifically for His calling on your life. Things that have happened which you thought might break you are what He'll use to make you into His special vessel to reach the world. Seek out His calling on your life. *Never underestimate what an extraordinary God can do through an ordinary person.* "For we are His workmanship, created in Christ Jesus for good works, which God prepared beforehand that we should walk in them" (Ephesians 2:10).

✦ **Listen for your calling:** Don't choose your calling, listen for it. Let God prepare you and guide you on the path He wants you to follow. You'll do more when you learn to wait upon His timing. We think we must get started sooner to get more done, but that's using worldly logic and not the wisdom from heaven. *You won't make a wrong turn when you're waiting on the Lord.* "Wait on the LORD, and keep His way, and He shall exalt you to inherit the land" (Psalm 37:34).

* **Step into your calling:** Believe in the dream God has given you. Let go of the things holding you back. Write down your vision and share your dream with a trusted friend. Establish in your mind today that you'll begin to press forward to the vision the Lord has given you. *When God gives you a dream, it's not for your entertainment.* "It will come about after this that I will pour out My Spirit on all mankind; and your sons and your daughters will prophesy, your old men will have dreams, your young men will see visions" (Joel 2:28 NASB).

3

Praying for a Miracle

If you need a miracle, just pray for one.

Peter told the beggar who was lame from birth, "I don't have any silver or gold! But I will give you what I do have. In the name of Jesus Christ from Nazareth, get up and start walking" (Acts 3:6 CEV).

IF YOU CAN BELIEVE God can perform a miracle, you'll press in and pray for it.

Do you believe in miracles? Do you believe the Lord can do the impossible before your very eyes? Our God is a miracle-breathing God. There's nothing too hard for Him. Our Lord spoke everything into existence, and our Lord breathed out stars across the expanse of the galaxies. Too often, we think too little of what God can do because we think too much about our own limitations. Stop limiting your prayers to your Father in heaven by the limits of what you can do.

Pray to God's limits, not yours. "For with God nothing shall be impossible" (Luke 1:37 KJV).

Many will look to the Lord to perform a miracle before they'll believe. And it's in their unbelief that the Lord will not do a miracle for them. Even if God did a miracle for them, they'd soon demand another. We can't treat God like a genie in a bottle and expect Him to treat us as if we were His master. God doesn't answer to us; we answer to Him. God doesn't need to prove Himself, and you should never ask Him to. Our part is only to believe He can do anything; He will take it from there.

The first step to walking in miracles is believing that you can. "Yeshua said to him, 'As far as possibilities go, everything is possible for the person who believes'" (Mark 9:23 NOG).

We often miss the miracle because it lacks the majesty and wonder we think a miracle must have. We think a miracle has to be something so grand that all the world looks in amazement. Yet the Lord isn't limited in the size of the miracles He performs by the expectations of those on earth. Sometimes the miracles are little in size, but the result is a huge blessing, and we can only stand in awe of the Father as He performs them.

Some of God's miracles are such small things by the measure of man. Elijah was on the run and needed something to eat. "Suddenly an angel touched him, and said to him, 'Arise and eat.' Then he looked, and there by his head was a cake baked on coals, and a jar of water" (1 Kings 19:5-6).

Sometimes we think that to be effective for the kingdom we must be the conduit of miracles for the kingdom. We think the person by whom the miracles will flow is somehow of greater worth than others who only pray for all that God would do. There's no difference in worth for any of the saints when they serve in the kingdom. As long as you seek credit for a miracle, your heavenly Father will choose someone else. The miracles are from heaven, the credit is only to God, and only the humble will be used to deliver them.

He often works from the realm of the impossible just so you can't take the credit. "Jesus looked at them and said, 'With people [as far as it depends on them] it is impossible, but with God all things are possible'" (Matthew 19:26 AMP).

We think that praying for a miracle is of value only if the miracle comes to pass. But we must trust our Father in however He chooses to answer a prayer. Pray for a miracle and let the cards fall as they will. Our heavenly Father knows what He's doing, and we must trust Him in all that He does. Keep praying for a miracle whether it happens or not, and you'll be a blessing to those you're praying for.

Faith believes that God can do anything even if He doesn't. "Now faith is the certainty of things hoped for, a proof of things not seen" (Hebrews 11:1 NASB).

I remember one time speaking with my family when my father had been having terrible pain for months. We'd all prayed that God would do a miracle and lift all pain from him. Not long after this, he went into the hospital and received some care for something unrelated to his pain. After he was released from the hospital, all the pain that he had from before was gone. Some were thinking the care must have helped. I remember saying, "Or it could be that God did a miracle and answered all our prayers."

There would be more prayers answered if more prayers were given. Jesus taught that we "always ought to pray and not lose heart" (Luke 18:1).

We often pray for a miracle, and if there's a blessing, we seek to give people credit where we can. If a prayer is answered and a miracle is performed, then give credit to the Lord. Even if someone helped to bring the healing, they were merely the instruments of God's grace. Pray for the miracle you need God to do, and let Him decide how He'll do it.

There's no limit to the power of God but only in our ability to believe. "Then the Lord said to Moses, 'Has my arm lost its power? Now you will see whether or not my word comes true!'" (Numbers 11:23 NLT).

The maturity of your faith and your walk with the Lord is revealed in how you see miracles. If you think something is beyond praying for, you don't yet know the endless power of our Almighty Father. If you think the Lord must perform a miracle to prove Himself to you, you don't yet know the simple truth that the heavens have already declared His glory. If you think that God must perform a miracle to be a good God, then you don't know God, for God is always a good God. Your confidence and trust in the Lord are the measure of your faith.

The level of our faith is revealed in the confidence we have as we pray for things. Jesus taught, "I tell you, you can pray for anything, and if you believe that you've received it, it will be yours" (Mark 11:24 NLT).

Pray for miracles with the faith as a child that your Father could do them. Learn to trust God in your prayers, knowing that He's faithful. Thank the Lord before He answers a prayer, and learn to praise Him no matter how He responds. Believe that God can do what you pray for, and don't agonize over whether or not He will. Don't lower your prayers, thinking that the Lord needs an easier goal to be successful. Trust your heavenly Father in His answers while praying fervently for the outcome you desire in your heart.

Stop being such a grown-up Christian and learn to pray like a little child. Jesus promised, "Whatever things you ask in prayer, believing, you will receive" (Matthew 21:22).

Several years ago, I was in a writing ministry to prisoners. I met a mother online at a prison ministry website and she asked me to do her a favor. Her name was Silvana and she lived in New York. Her son had been put in prison with a few years left to go. Silvana wanted me to write to him and help him grow in his faith. It was a privilege to do this, so I began writing to him. This is a passion of mine—to pour into people and teach them what it means to be a person of faith and honor. Specifically with men, I want to call them up to the type of man God intends for them to be, with a high character and a deep sense of duty.

The more you pour out, the more full you'll be. "And don't forget to do good and to share with those in need. These are the sacrifices that please God" (Hebrews 13:16 NLT).

As the months went by, I also corresponded with Silvana online. Her son never wrote me back, but he told her of some of the things I was telling him in the letters. Sometimes she let me know what he'd said to her. This was an encouragement for me to keep writing to him. I was so impressed by this mother's love for her son. Silvana would make long, difficult travels by bus to visit him. Adversity is a great teacher for growing in our faith.

God puts His saints through their trials to grow them. "We can rejoice, too, when we run into problems and trials, for we know that they are good for us—they help us learn to be patient. And patience develops strength of character in us and helps us trust God more each time we use it until finally our hope and faith are strong and steady" (Romans 5:3-4 TLB).

One day Silvana messaged me a draft of a prayer she wanted to pray to God. In this prayer she poured out her heart and her desire to have her son released from prison. It was very raw, blunt, and uncensored. I told her that I thought this is precisely the kind of prayer the Lord would want her to give. How much we need to open our hearts to our Father, by which He can then fill our heart with His love and His comfort!

The most productive time of your day is when you're praying. The Lord Jesus promised us, "You can ask for anything in my name, and I will do it, so that the Son can bring glory to the Father. Yes, ask me for anything in my name, and I will do it!" (John 14:13-14 NLT).

Silvana ended up printing out this prayer and pinning it to a wall above a shelf. On the shelf, she lit a candle. She was a Catholic, and most certainly, Catholics love to use candles. What a glorious image a candle has—a selfless light shining hope in a darkened world. Perhaps more of us would benefit from using candles in our prayer and worship.

You cannot have a light on and remain in the dark. Likewise, if Christ is in you, Christ will change you. Jesus said, "I am the light of the world. He who follows Me shall not walk in darkness, but have the light of life" (John 8:12).

Seven days later, Silvana was looking across the room at her prayer pinned to the wall with the candle burning just below it. Suddenly, the candle went out. At that very moment, the phone rang, and it was her son. He told her of a great miracle—they were releasing him early from prison. He'd be home in just a few short days. Her prayer had been answered.

We must remember that when we pray to God, there's nothing we ask for that He can't do. Jesus prayed, "Abba, Father, all things are possible for You" (Mark 14:36).

In whatever you're praying for, trust that the Lord can hear you, and believe that He can do anything. Don't worry about grammar or style in how you pray; just tell Him how you feel from the heart that He's given you. God loves you. God cares about you. No matter what your circumstances are, He's able to deliver you by His great and mighty hand.

The path to God is through prayer. "You will call upon Me and go and pray to Me, and I will listen to you. And you will seek Me and find Me, when you search for Me with all your heart" (Jeremiah 29:12-13).

Prayers

✦ *Heavenly Father, You know of everything I need before I could even ask for it. Nothing is impossible for You, and nothing escapes Your perfect attention to my life.*

✦ *Lord Jesus, You can calm a raging sea, and You can raise someone from the dead. Let me never doubt that You can help me in everything that I pray for.*

✦ *Holy Spirit, help me in my prayers to never pray below the unlimited power of all that the Father can do, and to have faith that He'll always do the perfect thing at the perfect time.*

Spiritual Growth

✦ **Pray as big as God is:** You must never see a problem as being too big for God. He's able to do more than we can ever ask or think, so just ask beyond what's reasonable, then let God decide what to do with it. *For the impossible to happen, we have to pray believing for the impossible.* Jesus said, "If you have faith as a mustard seed, you will say to this mountain, 'Move from here to there,' and it will move; and nothing will be impossible for you" (Matthew 17:20).

✦ **Pray with perseverance:** Praying with confidence comes after we learn to pray with perseverance. In the consistent perseverance of your prayers, the Lord will show up to meet you. *The more prayer you add to your life, the more your life has the fullness of God. It's by prayer that you can reach God; likewise, it's by prayer that God can reach you.* "Pray in the Spirit at all times and on every occasion. Stay alert and be persistent in your prayers for all believers everywhere" (Ephesians 6:18 NLT).

✴ **Believe for your miracle:** Learn to believe in God for the miracles you need. Believe that God can make a way, then leave it up to Him to determine how to do it. Surrender to the Lord so that He has His way with you. *If your circumstances didn't look so hopeless, His miracles wouldn't seem nearly as grand.* "You are the God of miracles and wonders! You still demonstrate your awesome power" (Psalm 77:14 TLB).

4

Trust Me

You don't have to understand God to trust Him.

"Though He slay me, yet will I trust Him"
(Job 13:15).

IF YOU CAN BELIEVE the Father is trustworthy in all things, you'll trust Him with whatever situation you find yourself in.

On our money we have the message "In God We Trust," yet we worry as if He's not with us. It's one thing to say you trust God and another to step out in faith and let Him carry you. We're much better at claiming a faith than walking in it. I propose to you that it's more worthwhile to live a small faith than to talk a big one.

Live your life during the week so that you could preach it on Sunday morning. "Be an example to the believers in word, in conduct, in love, in spirit, in faith, in purity" (1 Timothy 4:12).

It's important for you to tell the Lord what you're having a hard time trusting Him with. You may as well be honest with Him, because He knows when you're not. If you want to get closer to God, you have to be more real with Him. We always share the most with those we trust the most. You can always trust your Father enough to tell Him how you feel. What you tell your Father reveals the level of your closeness with Him.

Stop praying like an orphan; rather, pray as a child of God. "And because we are his children, God has sent the Spirit of his Son into our hearts, prompting us to call out, 'Abba, Father.' Now you are no longer a slave but God's own child. And since you are his child, God has made you his heir" (Galatians 4:6-7 NLT).

I was born with a cruel error in my sensory system in which many sights and sounds cause me pain. It's a subset of the conditions autistic people have. It makes it hard to be around people. Because of that, I've always been a loner. People don't understand this condition, and so I rarely speak of it. Before I was saved, I used to think that either there wasn't a God, or He was not a loving God—or else why would He have done this to me? He showed me later that through my suffering He was drawing me to Himself. The Lord always has a reason behind our suffering.

Learn to let suffering complete its work in you before God might remove it. "After you have suffered for a little while, the God of all grace [who imparts His blessing and favor], who called you to His own eternal glory in Christ, will Himself complete, confirm, strengthen, and establish you [making you what you ought to be]" (1 Peter 5:10 AMP).

Early on in my faith, I didn't understand this truth about the value in suffering. Yet all I wanted to do was serve Him. *Oh, what a work He does in us in our circumstances! Sometimes we think He's either absent or reckless in the process. It's only in hindsight that we can see things from His viewpoint.* Though we may not understand His ways, we can always trust Him. Though we may not agree with Him in the process, we'll all someday praise Him for all that He's done.

Trusting God doesn't mean you understand your circumstances, but only that you know He'll carry you through them. "And the LORD shall help them and deliver them; He shall deliver them from the wicked, and save them, because they trust in Him" (Psalm 37:40).

The Lord had called me to write letters to prisoners. This seemed a reasonable calling, considering how I loved to write and I could do it without being around others. It made sense to me that my heavenly Father knows my limitations and would call me to something I could comfortably do. But after writing to prisoners for many years, I had the leading of the Lord to go inside prisons to serve. I wasn't sure how I was supposed to serve, but I felt the leading—more like a great burden—of the Lord pressing me to go into prisons.

Stop thinking of your calling as a suggestion but a commandment of God. "For the gifts and the calling of God are irrevocable" (Romans 11:29).

I signed up for an orientation class for prison ministry. It was offered by Prison Fellowship, the same ministry I'd served in for years. This ministry was founded by Chuck Colson, who'd been a lawyer for President Nixon, and ended up in prison after the Watergate scandal. Mr. Colson was saved just before he went to prison, and it was there God gave him a ministry that he would lead for the rest of his life.

You'll hear the higher calling only when you're sitting in the lowest place. The Lord Jesus taught, "When you are invited, go and sit down in the lowest place" (Luke 14:10). *He was speaking not about good etiquette at a banquet, but about a way of life that leads to the higher calling.*

The orientation program was scheduled for two parts, the first on Friday evening, then an all-day session on Saturday. The Friday evening program was impossibly painful because of my sensory condition. This was the same reason I'd dropped out of school and avoided churches—being around groups is often impossible for me. This is why all my life I've spent most of my time alone. Nothing is by chance, and God can use everything for His purposes.

What matters most is not how much you understand God, but how much you trust Him. "Lean on, trust in, and be confident in the Lord with all your heart and mind and do not rely on your own insight or understanding" (Proverbs 3:5 AMPC).

The next morning, I headed out for the second full day of training. I was driving in my pickup truck through a very heavy rainstorm. This was an El Niño year—the rainstorms were fierce, and the freeways were flooded. As I drove down the freeway, the last thing I wanted to do was to go back to this training program and be in pain from being around all the people. I've always found this to be a cruel reality—that I love people so much, but often struggle to be around them.

Trust God's plans more than your feelings. "The counsel of the Lord stands forever, the plans of His heart to all generations" (Psalm 33:11).

I started praying out loud to God. I was asking Him why He was pressuring me to serve inside prisons. Why me? I didn't know the Bible that well, and my faith was not yet strong. Worst of all, He knew how hard it was for me to be around people. The more I was asking Him about these things, the angrier I became. I remember yelling at Him: "You can't ask me to do this! I don't know enough. I'm not good enough. I can't speak in front of people. I can't even be around people. You know I can't do this! You're the one that broke me. How dare You ask me!" I slammed my fist on the steering wheel.

The purposes of God are never limited by the abilities of man. Our full experience as believers is "predestined according to the purpose of Him who works all things according to the counsel of His will" (Ephesians 1:11).

Right then, my truck hit a pothole on the freeway, and the truck started hydroplaning out of control. I was really frightened, going so fast and not having any control. I'd just yelled at God, and now it seemed like He was going to make me pay for it. This situation was my life story—always out of control.

Then it happened, and my life was forever changed. For the first time, I clearly heard the voice of the Lord. It was more than the whispers into my heart that I had heard from the Lord before. This was strong. This was sure. He said only two words: "Trust Me." At that very moment, the truck regained control, and I drove straight ahead to the class.

It's easy to trust God until you really have to, and this is where the lesson begins. "And those who know Your name will put their trust in You, for You, Lord, have not abandoned those who seek You" (Psalm 9:10 NASB).

There was a longer journey for me after this before I started to go inside prisons. But those two words— "Trust Me"—stayed with me and carried me to do all that He ever asked me to do.

Fast-forward a few years later, and I was standing in front of seventy men inside a prison chapel. I preached my first message, which I called "In God We Trust." I carry a copy of that message in my Bible to this day.

I went on to preach a hundred messages and teach hundreds of more classes in several prisons. Sometimes the situations in prison ministry were impossibly painful for me, but I trusted the Lord to help me, and He always did.

The Lord being with you is never based on how you feel, but what He promises. Let your faith be what you know and not how you feel. "The Lord is trustworthy in all he promises and faithful in all he does. The Lord is near to all who call on him" (Psalm 145:13,18).

To this day, whenever I speak in front of others or write for the kingdom, I fall before the Lord and cry out to Him that I can't do it on my own. Then I surrender all and trust Him to do a work through me. No matter your obstacles, you can always trust God. His calling on your life is not by your abilities but by His. If we want to do more for the Lord, we must believe and trust that He will help us.

You can trust the Lord. There's nothing you can't entrust to a perfectly trustworthy heavenly Father.

Higher faith is not from knowing more, but from trusting more. "The Lord is my rock, my fortress, and my savior; my God is my rock, in whom I find protection. He is my shield, the power that saves me, and my place of safety" (Psalm 18:2 NLT).

When the Father calls His children to serve, He often asks them to do the impossible. He does this so that He can test you to see how much you'll trust Him. He called Abraham out of his country to go somewhere unknown. He called Moses to go up against the greatest nation of that day in Egypt. He called the young shepherd boy David to go up against the giant Goliath.

What impossible thing is He calling for you to do? What impossible dreams has He planted in your heart? It's impossible only if we try to do it without God. It will happen only when we come to trust Him with all our heart. Be willing to do what God is asking you to do.

Sometimes God won't part the sea until we trust Him to do it. "And the Lord said to Moses, 'Why do you cry to Me? Tell the children of Israel to go forward'" (Exodus 14:15).

If you want to believe for more, you must trust Him for more. If you want to believe for a miracle, you must trust that He can do a miracle. There's nothing impossible for God—but will you trust Him to that degree?

Listen for His voice. Press in to hear what He might say. Pay attention when you reach that day and that voice from heaven speaks to you and says, "Trust Me." Your faith will be revealed in how you answer Him.

If you walk beneath your calling, you won't accomplish all He has for you. "And Abram [later named Abraham] believed God; then God considered him righteous on account of his faith" (Genesis 15:6 TLB).

Prayers

✴ *Heavenly Father, help me to see all the ways in which You can use suffering for my benefit. Help me to look for and to see the purposes in everything I'm going through.*

✴ *Lord Jesus, You gave Your life to save my life, and I pray You would help me learn to trust You with all my life. Show me, Lord, how to trust You even when it doesn't make sense.*

✴ *Holy Spirit, I fall down before You, helpless and needy, broken and weary—and I pray that You'll help me. Be the strength and the song in me, and help me serve Jesus with all my life.*

Spiritual Growth

✴ **Serve in the small things:** The Lord has a calling on your life. He has a purpose and a plan to get you there. Learn to trust Him in His timing and accept whatever He asks you to do. *He will not give you a bigger calling until you first walk in the smaller one.* The Lord Jesus taught, "He who is faithful in what is least is faithful also in much" (Luke 16:10). *The test is always in the least.*

✴ **Pray with a purpose:** Start praying with a passion and with a purpose. Be specific in what you pray for, and expect Him to answer you. Seek His will, and when you find it, the windows of heaven will be opened. *Your expectations toward God are the measure of your faith in God. When you pray for rain, do you bring an umbrella?* "Now to him who by his power working in us is able to do far beyond anything we can ask or imagine, to him be glory" (Ephesians 3:20-21 CJB).

✦ **Trust that He has you:** In whatever you've gone through and whatever you're going through now, learn to give it all over to Jesus. Let Him be your hiding place and your refuge, and trust that He'll never leave you. *For some of our troubles, the only thing we can say is Selah.* "You are my hiding place; You shall preserve me from trouble; You shall surround me with songs of deliverance. *Selah*" (Psalm 32:7). Selah is not a word to say but a call for us to take pause and to reflect on what God is saying in His Word.

5

Effective Prayers

If you're a believer, then pray like one.

Jesus promised us: "Everything you ask for in prayer will be yours, if you only have faith" (Mark 11:24 CEV).

IF YOU CAN BELIEVE that God can do anything and that He'll always do the right thing, you'll pray for everything, trusting Him with however He might answer.

We think that an effective prayer is one in which the Lord immediately gives us what we ask for. But this is a measurement on the scales of man and not from the courts of heaven. We imagine that if we pray better, we'll get better answers. But we're wrong. Our heavenly Father always has the best answers regardless of how poorly we might pray.

The secret of prayer is in knowing our complete dependence upon God. "God said to me once and for all, 'All the strength and power you need flows from me!'" (Psalm 62:11 TPT).

An effective prayer has nothing to do with how the Lord might answer and everything to do with how much the saints pour out their heart and entrust everything to their loving heavenly Father. An effective prayer is one in which the saint simply makes his or her request known to God and trusts that God will answer every prayer in the right way, at the right time, and for the right reasons.

It's when we pray from our heart that we can touch the heart of God. "Blessed and favored by God are those who keep His testimonies, and who [consistently] seek Him and long for Him with all their heart" (Psalm 119:2 AMP).

Stop trying to impress the Lord Jesus with how talented you are in your praying, and simply fall down at His feet and let Him know how you really feel. You can never fool the Lord, so don't try. Your intimacy with Christ Jesus is proven in how open you are with Him in your private moments. He loves you unconditionally, so pray without worrying that you need to impress Him. He'll be impressed by nothing less than your genuineness.

Secret prayers impress God more because they aren't trying to impress other people. Jesus taught us to pray: "When you pray, go into your room, and when you have shut your door, pray to your Father who is in the secret place; and your Father who sees in secret will reward you openly" (Matthew 6:6).

The Lord is not auditioning for actors, but seeking those who trust Him enough to share their heart with Him. If you don't trust the Lord with your heart, He knows it. He already knows what's in your heart, so you may as well just tell Him. It's not that you're telling Him something He doesn't know; rather, you're proving that you trust Him with all your secrets.

The best prayer you can offer to the Lord is the one already written on your heart. The Lord Jesus said, "The hour is coming, and now is, when the true worshipers will worship the Father in spirit and truth; for the Father is seeking such to worship Him" (John 4:23).

When I'd first gone through the orientation at Prison Fellowship, they asked us to fill out a form so we could get admitted to their program. One item on the form asked for a pastor's recommendation. Being that I was a loner, the pastors at my church had no idea who I was. So I met with one of them, and he insisted that I join several small groups and Bible studies there at the church before he would recommend me. I did as he required, though with my sensory condition it was always extremely hard to go to these programs.

Never set your goals based on the difficulties you may face, but on the promises you'll walk in. "You must not fear them, for the LORD your God Himself fights for you" (Deuteronomy 3:22).

Even though being in the programs was hard, I was blessed by them. I spent three years doing many Bible study classes and social gatherings, learning and growing in my faith along the way. I was also learning how to be around people. I never did great, but I got better. I met so many wonderful souls who poured into my life and blessed me with their words of wisdom. I met some special saints whose influence changed me forever. God arranges such wonderful things for those who follow Him.

Where streams meet, rivers begin. We need each other. "Two are better than one.... For if they fall, one will lift up his companion" (Ecclesiastes 4:9-10).

Too often, people rush into ministry without allowing God to first prepare them for all He will have them do. They rush ahead of God's will and operate from their own imperfect passions. They'll pick their own calling instead of waiting and listening for what He would call them to do. The call of God is never spoken by our own mouth. The calling includes not only *what* to do but also *when*. Moses needed forty years to prepare—so why are you in such a hurry? We shouldn't try to direct or rush our eternal Father, who alone understands the best path and the best time for His children to do ministry.

The secret to being led by the Lord is waiting on the Lord. "The LORD is good to those who wait for Him, to the person who seeks Him" (Lamentations 3:25 NASB).

After three years of involvement in these programs at my church and learning how to be around people, it was finally time. I asked the pastor if he would now recommend me. I think he was surprised that I'd persevered and done everything he told me to do, and had waited so long before asking him again. He was pleased to write a letter of recommendation for me.

Child of God, if we won't submit before our church leaders, it only reveals the rebelliousness in our hearts. Your submission to the leaders of your church is where your submission to God is proven.

To the degree you won't submit to authority, rebellion still reigns in you. "Obey your spiritual leaders, and do what they say. Their work is to watch over your souls, and they are accountable to God" (Hebrews 13:17 NLT).

I checked in with the leadership of Prison Fellowship and learned that I needed to go through another training program. So I signed up to go to one of these trainings. A few weeks before the class, I woke up one morning and was struggling with my failures before God. I wanted to live higher than I did, but I didn't know how to get there. Before I left for work, I knelt down in my garage next to my motorcycle. I don't remember all the words I spoke in that prayer, but I clearly remember the last words I prayed to God: "Father, I want You to shake up my life and draw me closer to Yourself."

A few hours later, I was in a motorcycle wreck.

It's in the hardest of times that God does the greatest work in the heart of a man or a woman. "Dear brothers, is your life full of difficulties and temptations? Then be happy, for when the way is rough, your patience has a chance to grow. So let it grow, and don't try to squirm out of your problems. For when your patience is finally in full bloom, then you will be ready for anything, strong in character, full and complete" (James 1:2-4 TLB).

Immediately after the wreck, I thought of my prayer and told God, "Not like that." I had busted up my leg and foot really bad. I was in such terrible pain. Some people say we should be careful what we pray for. I say we should be reckless in our prayers, knowing our heavenly Father will only do what's best for us. Sometimes the worst things that can happen to us will cause the best results.

Sometimes the Lord has to hurt you to help you. "Young man, do not resent it when God chastens and corrects you, for his punishment is proof of his love. Just as a father punishes a son he delights in to make him better, so the LORD corrects you" (Proverbs 3:11-12 TLB).

I want you to know that God answered every bit of my prayer. He shook up my life, and He drew me closer to Himself. The Lord taught me how to pray during this time like I'd never prayed before. I was in so much pain from my injuries that I had to cancel going to the next prison training program. But my Father had placed me into a training program of His own. Often the Lord must disrupt your plans so that you'll step into His.

An effective prayer never depends upon you. "Since we have this confidence, we can also have great boldness before him, for if we present any request agreeable to his will, he will hear us" (1 John 5:14 TPT).

The most effective prayer you can say will be the one that wrecks your natural life the most. Our heavenly Father's plans will trump the ideals of this world. His ways are so much higher that we simply can't grasp them. If you pray believing, your faith will open up the way. If you pray in His will, your words will open the windows of heaven. Believe for more and seek His will, then pray as if the answer has already come.

An effective prayer is spoken believing that God can do anything. The secret to an effective prayer is never in the answer, but in your faith as you're praying. The Lord Jesus promised, "If you live in me and what I say lives in you, then ask for anything you want, and it will be yours" (John 15:7 NOG).

Too many try to pray using words they think God wants to hear. They think the eloquence of their speech plays into the outcome of their prayers. You can't manipulate the Lord with your choice of words, and you can't sway Him by your speaking skills. Effective prayers will sound like you're speaking to a trusted friend. An effective prayer doesn't mask the person but reveals their heart. God is looking for people to be real with Him.

It's to our detriment that we don't think of prayer as a conversation but as an exhortation. "Each morning you listen to my prayer, as I bring my requests to you and wait for your reply" (Psalm 5:3 CEV).

When I asked the Lord to do whatever He wanted to do in my life, He most certainly did. And though it hurt me a great deal, it actually healed me. It's in our brokenness that He can form us into something new. Our heavenly Father wants to bring about a change in us. He wants us to believe that He can, and then to trust Him in the process.

Don't imagine an easy path when you're doing work for the Lord here on this earth. The greater your calling, the harder the road will be.

The holier the man, the more convicted is his soul. The Lord Jesus said, "And when He [the Holy Spirit] has come, He will convict the world of sin" (John 16:8). *Apart from conviction, the sin remains the same. The road to holiness is only through the deep valley of conviction.*

Pray believing and pray expecting. Pray your heart, and you'll be speaking to His heart.

Your Father loved you enough to send His Son to die for you while you were still His enemy. No matter what you share with Him from your heart, never think that He won't love you. Be real with your Father and tell Him how you're feeling. Be honest in where you're failing. It's your trust in His mercy to tell Him anything that will make your life useful for the kingdom of God.

It does not matter as much how many times you fall, but how many times you get back up. "Even if good people fall seven times, they will get back up" (Proverbs 24:16 CEV).

Prayers

✢ *Heavenly Father, I want to open up my heart to You and tell You how I'm feeling. I want to share my innermost thoughts with You, knowing how very much You love me.*

✢ *Lord Jesus, I want to learn to pray like You prayed, pouring out Your heart to the Father, all alone on the mountaintop, late into the night.*

✢ *Holy Spirit, teach me to pray the words written on my heart and prepared for heaven, so that the Father hears me. Teach me to know His will so that my prayers will land there.*

Spiritual Growth

✢ **Pray more:** If you want to have a higher faith, you must live a life of prayer. We get nearest to our Father on our knees, and we're led by Him from within our prayer closets. There's no greater thing you can do to become higher in your faith than to spend more time in prayer. *When your life is a prayer, the Lord will always be near you.* "Make your life a prayer" (1 Thessalonians 5:17 TPT).

✦ **Pray to be changed:** Be daring in your requests to your Father. Be willing to give up the right to yourself and give over to the Lord the right to do with you as He pleases. In your prayers, declare Him the Lord over your life, then ask Him to change you forever. *Would you ever pray, "God, do whatever it takes for me to grow closer to You"? Maybe you fear that He may have to hurt you to accomplish this. The truth for some is that He may have to hurt them. But He has to take by force only that which you refuse to surrender.* "Search me, O God, and know my heart; test me and know my anxious thoughts. Point out anything in me that offends you, and lead me along the path of everlasting life" (Psalm 139:23-24 NLT).

✦ **Pray believing:** Learn to believe in the unchanging power of God. When you read about miracles in Holy Scripture, just believe that He can do the same today. The people whom God used in that day were no different than you or me. They only believed, and we must do the same. *It's not what you know that Jesus is interested in, but what you believe.* Jesus asks us this question: "When the Son of Man returns, how many will he find on the earth who have faith?" (Luke 18:8 NLT). *Knowledge says that mountains can be moved; faith moves them.*

6

A Step of Faith

*We don't need to know the end of
God's plan to step into it.*

"By faith Abraham obeyed when he was called to go out to the place which he would receive as an inheritance. And he went out, not knowing where he was going" (Hebrews 11:8).

**IF YOU CAN BELIEVE that God can always help you,
you'll step into whatever He's calling you to do,
fully trusting that He has you.**

We're often faced with challenges to our faith. We come up against something, and we have a choice: We either take a step of faith, or we sit down. How easy it is to claim an unstoppable faith so long as nothing arises that might stop it. Yet it's in the barriers to our faith that our faith can rise even higher. It takes a reason to have faith in order to develop a stronger faith.

Until your faith is your life, it's only an accessory. "Look at the proud one, his soul is not right within him, but the righteous will live by his faith [in the true God]" (Habakkuk 2:4 AMP).

There's a teaching in our day that when the Lord closes one door, He'll open another. That's sometimes true, yet I believe the Lord often closes a door to see if we have the fire and the determination to keep knocking. Sometimes it's those who keep pounding on the door who are firmly in the will of God. Jesus didn't say to knock only once; He said, "To him who keeps knocking, the door will be opened" (Matthew 7:8 CJB).

Stop imagining a God who makes things easy for His servants. Consider the lives of His prophets; not one of them had an easy life. The test of our faith will be in how we respond to the obstacles He allows to come up against us. Sometimes the path of least resistance will take you straight into a disaster. Wide and easy is the road to hell, so we need to look for the narrow path. Don't look for the easy way, but ask Him to show you the right way—the way He would have you go.

If your journey is easy, you might be on the wrong road. The Lord Jesus taught, "Go in through the narrow gate. The gate to destruction is wide, and the road that leads there is easy to follow. A lot of people go through that gate. But the gate to life is very narrow. The road that leads there is so hard to follow that only a few people find it" (Matthew 7:13-14 CEV).

I'd been in a season of preparation from the Lord as I was healing from my motorcycle accident. My left leg and foot were fractured and beat up really bad. I had to go with no weight on that leg for two months. I'd canceled my prison training course because the pain was simply too great to go anywhere. There was no knocking the door down in this season, but only a time to heal and pray that the Lord Jesus would help me. Too often, we wait for trouble to start praying more, when we should pray more before the trouble even comes.

Father, I want my prayer life to be such that in the greatest trials, my time with You need not increase, but only change subjects for a time. "The LORD gives perfect peace to those whose faith is firm" (Isaiah 26:3 CEV).

I signed up for the next prison ministry class held a few months later, and I was so blessed to finally be on the path to where the Lord was leading me. When I went for the training, it was still really hard to get around. I couldn't wear shoes because of the swelling in my foot. I was wearing a brace on my leg. Yet when the Lord calls, we need to answer, whether or not we feel ready. We need to stop looking for excuses not to go, and instead start rebuking the obstacles that stand before us.

You'll start making progress when you stop making excuses. "Farmers who wait for perfect weather never plant. If they watch every cloud, they never harvest" (Ecclesiastes 11:4 NLT).

After a day and a half of training, there were signup sheets laid out for different prison events we could choose to be part of. I was still in no condition to go into a prison, since getting around on crutches was incredibly hard. It was all I could do to go even short distances. I couldn't put any pressure on my leg yet, and it had weakened with atrophy from not being used for a few months. All my toes were fractured, purple, and swollen. I'd sustained permanent nerve damage in my foot that made it hurt and feel very strange. But I took a step of faith and signed up for a prison program to be held several weeks later.

You have to take a step of faith to walk in the kingdom life. "For we live by believing and not by seeing" (2 Corinthians 5:7 NLT).

The troubles you're going through are the things your Father is using to prepare you. Circumstances are the hammer and chisel God uses to form you. Adversity is the classroom where you're given the chance to learn the most difficult lessons. I don't know what you're going through, but your heavenly Father does. My prayer for you is that you'll trust Him even when you don't understand what He's doing. The Father's plans are perfect even when we suffer.

When God has you on your knees, it's there He can change you. "'Can I not do with you as this potter?' says the Lord. 'Look, as the clay is in the potter's hand, so are you in My hand'" (Jeremiah 18:6).

When the time was drawing near to go into prison, I still couldn't get around without crutches. I couldn't go into the prison with crutches, so I was praying that God would help me. I prayed all the way up to the day and the minute before entering the prison. The Lord made a way. My first day walking without crutches was in the prison ministry that the Lord had called me into many years before. We spent the whole day going unit to unit, helping men sign up their children to receive Christmas gifts through the Angel Tree program. I was limping and in pain, walking very slowly, but I was so filled with the hope of what God was doing in my life. There in the midst of the prison, I knew this was the ministry I belonged in.

When our faith rises, so does our reliance upon His power. "For the Lord your God is He who goes with you, to fight for you against your enemies, to save you" (Deuteronomy 20:4). *Never limit your faith to what you can do.*

Some of the people I ministered with that day have remained my friends many years later, and they continue to be a blessing in my life. Often when God calls us to do ministry, He places us where others can minister into our lives. Stop imagining that you'll be the only one blessing others, and you'll find those the Lord has put there to bless you. It's never by accident that the Lord places those souls in your path.

Your life is a brushstroke of God on the canvas from heaven that displays His mercy here on earth. After saving a man, Jesus told him, "Go home to your own [family and relatives and friends] and bring back word to them of how much the Lord has done for you, and [how He has] had sympathy for you and mercy on you" (Mark 5:19 AMPC). *You were not saved to sit, but to serve.*

The prison we went into that day was the West Yard of the California Institution for Men. The following year we couldn't go into the West Yard because there'd been a terrible riot, and the inmates had burned many of the units to the ground. It took a few years to rebuild that yard, and for the last several years that I ministered in prisons, that was the yard I went into most often.

The Lord called me out of prison ministry after seven years so I could write, and it was that prison where He first had me go that I preached at for my last time. God arranges things in a way we could never imagine.

Your life is bigger than yourself because it touches everyone around you. "Let your light so shine before men, that they may see your good works and glorify your Father in heaven" (Matthew 5:16).

To this day, my foot feels very strange with every step I take because of the nerve damage. If I walk too much, it can start to hurt me. With every step, I'm reminded of the answered prayer from the Lord to shake up my life and draw me closer to Himself. With every step, I'm reminded of all He called me to do. With every step, I'm reminded of the great importance that we take a step of faith in the face of uncertainty.

Child of God, where do you need to take a step of faith? What is the Lord calling you to do? What will require the power of God for you to do it? Take a step of faith today.

Faith is not what you can do, but what you believe He can do. In Daniel 3, three young men facing certain death told Nebuchadnezzar, "If we are thrown into the blazing furnace, the God whom we serve is able to save us… But even if he doesn't, we want to make it clear to you, Your Majesty, that we will never serve your gods" (Daniel 3:17-18 NLT).

I see so many who don't take a step of faith because they want to see the end of the plan before they step into it. There's no faith in that line of thinking. God purposefully designs our calling to test our faith, because it's only in faith that we can rightly serve Him. God knows that until you trust Him, there's not much He can do with you. Take a step of faith, trusting your Father as His own child, knowing that He has you.

It's not the faith you claim, but the faith you live. It's not the mask you wear, but the man or woman you are. "Serve Him with a loyal heart and with a willing mind" (1 Chronicles 28:9).

Child of God, step into your calling, and use the faith God has given you. If you need more faith, just pray that He would give it to you. There are people on this planet counting on you. Take a step of faith. Trust in God. You'll serve Him with His qualifications, not yours. And once you take this step, you'll be a blessing to those around you, and a blessing to the kingdom of God. And always remember: *Go for high ground in your calling.*

We hurt the Lord when we walk beneath our calling. "Walk worthy of the calling with which you were called, with all lowliness and gentleness, with longsuffering, bearing with one another in love, endeavoring to keep the unity of the Spirit in the bond of peace" (Ephesians 4:1-3).

Prayers

✦ *Heavenly Father, give me the courage to take a step of faith in every new calling You have for me. Give me a measure of faith that can overcome every doubt my mind might think of.*

- *Lord Jesus, you walked in a faith that believed all things were possible, and so that's how You prayed. Help me in seeking to have a faith that You modeled so perfectly.*

- *Holy Spirit, teach me to have wisdom and courage in everything that stands before me. Guide me to be discerning of where You would have me go next.*

Spiritual Growth

- **The testing of your faith:** The Lord will test your faith. The testing is not to prove you wrong but to build you up with what's right. Sometimes we fail, and that's part of the lesson. Learn your lesson, then move on. *God must test your faith to reveal your faith.* "The purpose of these troubles is to test your faith as fire tests how genuine gold is" (1 Peter 1:7 NOG).

- **Start serving today:** While the Lord prepares you for what lies ahead, serve in some capacity where you are right now. *If you don't know your calling, just serve alongside somebody who does. If you won't do the least for God, then He won't do the most through you.* "Therefore, since we are receiving a kingdom which cannot be shaken, let us have grace, by which we may serve God acceptably with reverence and godly fear" (Hebrews 12:28).

- **Take a step of faith:** Stop waiting for everything to be so perfect that you don't need faith, because the Lord expects you to take a step of faith. Pray to your Father to show you where He wants you to go, then trust that He'll help you get there. *You won't reach new heights by sitting in your comfort zone.* "Have I not commanded you? Be strong and courageous! Do not be terrified or dismayed (intimidated), for the LORD your God is with you wherever you go" (Joshua 1:9 AMP).

7

Purposes of God

When you're walking in the purposes of God, it's by His hand that you'll prevail.

"I know that You can do everything, and that no purpose of Yours can be withheld from You" (Job 42:2).

IF YOU CAN BELIEVE God has a purpose for your life, you'll seek the purpose He has for you and step into it, knowing that He'll help you every step of the way.

The purposes of man are often flawed, even if the goals seem worthy. The problem is that we usually have wrong motives, and our perspective is always too limited. We think in our worldly minds that good plans should face few troubles. We take the path of least resistance, and we think ourselves clever in our planning. At the first sign of rejection or failure, we quickly change our route so we can think ourselves wise. But in the end, the purposes of man are often thwarted because they lack the direction and power of God.

You're either walking in the plans of man or the purposes of God. The difference is this: The purposes of God never fail. "Indeed for this purpose I have raised you up, that I may show My power in you, and that My name may be declared in all the earth" (Exodus 9:16).

The purposes of God are perfect and complete no matter how broken they may appear. The plans of God are unstoppable because they're backed by His power. There's no obstacle too big that the Father can't overcome. There's no surprising an eternal God who isn't bound by time or limited in knowledge. Our Father often chooses the impossible way so that we'll know that it's by His power alone that we can make it. God's purposes can't be thwarted, and His plans can't be undone. You must hold onto these truths when He calls you to serve in His kingdom.

Be a person God can use to build His kingdom. "If you stay away from sin you will be like one of these dishes made of purest gold—the very best in the house—so that Christ himself can use you for his highest purposes" (2 Timothy 2:21 TLB).

God has a purpose for you. He's preparing you for your purpose whether or not you know your purpose yet. If you don't yet know your purpose, then simply serve Him with every opportunity before you.

When you know your purpose and step into it, things will get hard for you. It's these hard times that will cause you to rely on the Lord the most. It's His divine plan that you need Him. Self-reliance is a worldly idea that needs to be cast out from the life of a believer. To serve God rightly, you need Him to help you. Stop trying to be good enough, and just surrender.

The Lord doesn't use you because you're worthy, but because you're willing. To be in His will, you must be willing. "Serve Yahweh wholeheartedly and willingly because he searches every heart and understands every thought we have" (1 Chronicles 28:9 NOG).

When the Lord gave me the purpose to serve Him inside prisons, at first I told Him no. I felt so completely unqualified to serve Him in this way. My broken sensory system should have disqualified me before such a ministry ever began. I lacked knowledge and social skills by any reasonable standard. I didn't know the Bible well enough to teach small children, let alone adults. In my mind, God couldn't have chosen a worse candidate. But God doesn't choose us because we're able, but only because we're willing. When once you surrender your life, it will be His.

With Christianity, you're either all in or you're not. "Jesus said to his disciples, 'If you truly want to follow me, you should at once completely reject and disown your own life. And you must be willing to share my cross and experience it as your own, as you continually surrender to my ways'" (Matthew 16:24 TPT).

Friend, God knows what He's doing. When He calls you to something, be sure that it's by His qualifications, not yours. Never think the way will get easy when you say yes, because it's just the opposite—things will get hard. When I said yes to His plans, the obstacles started to form. It took several years from the time He called me into prisons to the first time I stepped inside one. Without obstacles, we wouldn't need God, and He knows it. We need a Red Sea so that we'll witness the power of God to get us through it.

God didn't remove the obstacle of the Red Sea, but gave His people a way through it. "Are You not the One who dried up the sea, the waters of the great deep; that made the depths of the sea a road for the redeemed to cross over?" (Isaiah 51:10).

I started serving in a couple of prisons in various weekly and monthly programs they had going. Soon I started teaching and then preaching, which was much to my surprise. I felt so completely inadequate, and I threw myself before God that He might help me. He always helped me. There were many others who had far better skills in speaking and socializing with others. I was never popular and never much to look at. All I had was Jesus. I want you to know: If all you have is Jesus, that's enough.

The problem we have in ministry is that we have too many strong ministers. As the Lord Jesus said to Paul, "My grace is all you need. My power works best in weakness." And Paul's response was this: "So now I am glad to boast about my weaknesses, so that the power of Christ can work through me" (2 Corinthians 12:9 NLT).

After several months of serving, I applied to get a staff card at a large multi-prison complex called the California Institution for Men. This would allow me to go into the different prison yards unescorted and teach classes or preach services. I could then escort others into the prison who were volunteering for the day, or for a program that went on for several weeks. One night I was being escorted into the prison and we met the warden's community director just outside the gate. He saw me and called me over to him, then walked with me a short distance so we could speak in private. He told me that they'd checked my past and there's no way I would ever get a staff card for that prison. Then he turned around and left.

It's by His grace that our past is forgiven, and it's for His purposes that we press forward. "God...has saved us and called us with a holy calling, not according to our works, but according to His own purpose and grace which was given to us in Christ Jesus before time began" (2 Timothy 1:8-9).

I remember questioning God. Why did He call me to something I didn't want to do and wasn't qualified to do? Why did He give me the desire and confidence to step into it, only to have it ripped away by the power of man? I was so disheartened, thinking it was over before it began. I'd argued so long with God telling Him: "How dare You ask me to go into the prisons?"—and now He was making it where I couldn't serve Him in the very prisons He sent me into. My eyes were fixed on what man was saying.

The purposes of God are never dependent on the provisions of man. "Abraham named the place Yahweh-Yireh (which means 'the LORD will provide')" (Genesis 22:14 NLT).

A few weeks later, I was called by the state chaplain for this prison. He told me I'd been approved, and that I was to come up to the prison and visit the personnel office so they could issue me a staff card.

Friend, when the Lord calls us to something, it's by His power that things will come to pass. For the next several years, I continued to get my prison staff card renewed every year. There were challenges every year when I went to renew it, but the Lord always made a way.

If the Lord has given you a vision, then He will make a way. "Before we were even born, he gave us our destiny; that we would fulfill the plan of God who always accomplishes every purpose and plan in his heart" (Ephesians 1:11 TPT).

Several months after that experience, I was feeling more comfortable about serving the Lord Jesus in the purpose He'd called me to. But it seems that God doesn't let us get comfortable for very long. One weekend, I was asked to pick up a minister many miles from where I lived, and to drive him to the prison and then escort him inside to teach. He was a mountain of a man with such a confidence in himself. He spoke with so much authority and conviction. I felt low next to him, as if he belonged to a league I could never be promoted to. When I see the abilities in others, it makes me realize all the ways I'm lacking.

God's purposes for you don't depend on your abilities. "God has chosen the foolish things of the world to put to shame the wise, and God has chosen the weak things of the world to put to shame the things which are mighty" (1 Corinthians 1:27).

As we were driving to the prison, this man told me that I'd never be effective in prison ministry. He said I'd never reach the men because my race and background were different from many of the men there. His words shook me, because I wondered if his words were true. I'd not even wanted to serve except that the Lord had called me to it. But what if this man was right? What if I would never be effective? Often the greatest obstacles in our ministry are the people who serve in the ministry.

The call of God is never dependent on our abilities, but only on our willingness to serve. "For if there is first a willing mind, it is accepted according to what one has, and not according to what he does not have" (2 Corinthians 8:12).

Within a few weeks, this man dropped out of the ministry, while I went on to serve for many years after he left. I'm sure there were others more effective and far more popular than me in the prison ministry, but I know that the Lord Jesus worked through me to reach some. This is not to my promotion but to God's glory, for all that He can do through a life that's yielded over to Him. Over the years, I saw men and women getting healed, saved, and changed by the power of God.

Friend, don't let the rejection of man deter you from the purposes of God.

If God has called you to it, people need to just get out of the way. "The Lord of Heaven's Armies has spoken—who can change his plans? When his hand is raised, who can stop him?" (Isaiah 14:27 NLT).

I think back to this time when the prison official told me I'd never serve in that prison. God never failed me, and He'll never fail you. If the Lord calls you to something, you just need to trust Him and do it. Though the obstacles will come, learn to trust Him in your journey. Let the trials form you, and let the disappointments strengthen you. Wherever there's opposition, we have the power of God to help us through.

Every purpose spoken from heaven is fulfilled on earth. "So will My word be which goes out of My mouth; it will not return to Me empty, without accomplishing what I desire, and without succeeding in the purpose for which I sent it" (Isaiah 55:11 NASB).

I think back to the time when this man from the ministry told me I'd never be effective in prison ministry. He was right—I could never be effective, but Christ in me could. We think that it's in our own strength that the Lord Jesus can use us, but it's in our weakness before Him where He's our strength before others.

In whatever He's calling you to do, know that He's the one who's working through you.

Never fear the leading of the Lord but beware the deception of man. "Lead me in the right path, O LORD, or my enemies will conquer me. Make your way plain for me to follow" (Psalm 5:8 NLT).

Prayers

✢ *Heavenly Father, help me forgive those who've come against me, knowing that even in their actions Your plans will come to pass.*

✢ *Lord Jesus, help me not to be deterred when following You. Help me to stay in such close communion with You that I know I'm walking in the purposes You have for me.*

✢ *Holy Spirit, guide me in the way I should go. Help me hear You clearly as You lead me in the purposes of the Father and the perfect plans of Christ.*

Spiritual Growth

✢ **Be led by the Holy Spirit:** The Holy Spirit was sent to this earth in order to guide us and teach us in all that we do. Believe in the promises of God that the Holy Spirit can lead you. Pray each morning that the Holy Spirit will guide you throughout the day. *Get counsel from man, but be led only by the Holy Spirit.* Jesus promised us: "The Helper, the Holy Spirit, whom the Father will send in My name, He will teach you all things, and bring to your remembrance all things that I said to you" (John 14:26).

* **Depend on the Lord:** When you come up to your Red Sea, it's there that God will test you. The test is never to see if you're strong enough, but if you're weak enough before God. The sooner you learn to depend on the Lord, the fewer failures you'll have in your journey. *Spiritual power is hindered by natural efforts. The harder you try, the greater the hindrance. The most effective saints don't do the most—they simply have faith in the One who can.* The Lord Jesus said, "I can guarantee this truth: If your faith is the size of a mustard seed, you can say to this mountain, 'Move from here to there,' and it will move. Nothing will be impossible for you" (Matthew 17:20 NOG). *The secret to moving mountains is having faith in the One who can.*

* **Press into your purpose:** Once you know your purpose, press into it with all you've got. The obstacles you face always serve a purpose. They test your resolve and prepare you for bigger battles ahead. Learn to trust the Lord in the process, and don't lose heart along the way. Pray more than you worry, and trust more than you fear. *It's when you have to press in the hardest that He's doing the greatest work in you.* "We are hard-pressed on every side, yet not crushed; we are perplexed, but not in despair; persecuted, but not forsaken; struck down, but not destroyed" (2 Corinthians 4:8-9).

8

Saving Figaro

God is the power of prayer.

"And the prayer of faith will save the sick, and the Lord will raise him up" (James 5:15).

IF YOU CAN BELIEVE your Father can do anything, you'll come to Him as His child and simply ask Him for whatever it is you need.

Several years ago, my wife Mary was working as a teacher's aide at a Christian school our children were attending. One day some people there found a lost kitten. Nobody knew where it came from. They asked Mary if she wanted to take him home. She decided to rescue this little kitten. It was her first cat. He was a black and white tuxedo kitten, so she named him Figaro after the cat from the movie Pinocchio. She called him Figgy for short. She became very close with Figgy, and he adored her. God's creatures are such a wonderful gift for His children. He's our Father, we're His children, and He loves to give us blessings.

We must come to God as children, because He's our Father. "And because you are sons, God has sent forth the Spirit of His Son into your hearts, crying out, 'Abba, Father!'" (Galatians 4:6).

Figaro didn't care for me, and in truth, I didn't care for Figaro. I had a dog named Simone, and I liked my dog. One evening I let Simone in, and she went straight for the kitchen table, looking for any crumbs that had fallen to the floor. By this time, Mary had rescued another cat, and this new cat had kittens that were now running around our house. The kittens were all there under that table and started hissing at my dog even though my dog wasn't bothering them. Then Figaro came marching into the dining area, and even though he wasn't the father of these kittens, he was determined to protect them as if he was. He attacked my dog, and Simone let out a great yelp. I jumped up to intervene.

The drama wasn't over. Figaro was very mad and hissing at my dog. Simone was nervous and just wanted to get away. I motioned with my hand for Simone to go down the hall so I could put her out back. She was glad to leave. Right then, Figaro came flying through the air to attack her, and my hand was right in the way. His claws dug into my finger. I yelled at Figaro and he ran away. I went and made sure the dog was safely outside, then I came back looking for Figaro.

I was sure angry at Figaro. My dog had meant no harm. Figaro had gotten out of control, and when he clawed me, that was the last straw.

He'd moved to the far end of our living room. I walked up to the edge of the room. I remember yelling at him and seeing his big eyes looking back at me in fear. Just because we're saved doesn't mean we won't get angry. The question is: Will we hold onto our anger?

In the kingdom, kindness is a strength and anger is a weakness. "Since God chose you to be the holy people he loves, you must clothe yourselves with tenderhearted mercy, kindness, humility, gentleness, and patience" (Colossians 3:12 NLT).

From that day forward, Figaro and I were enemies. If I came into a room, he'd leave. If he came near me, I'd chase him away. He would meow annoyingly loud at me—purposefully to irritate me, I think—and I'd chase him upstairs or send him outside.

We lived like this for several years. I wanted nothing to do with him, and I'm certain he wanted nothing to do with me. It's amazing how broken relationships can go on so long because of how stubborn and unforgiving we are.

Until you forgive it, you'll continue to live it. "Get rid of your bitterness, hot tempers, anger, loud quarreling, cursing, and hatred. Be kind to each other, sympathetic, forgiving each other as God has forgiven you through Christ" (Ephesians 4:31-32 NOG).

I'll never forget one summer afternoon when I was in the kitchen at the sink. Figaro was outside that day, and he jumped up on the shelf just outside the kitchen window. I had the hose sprayer to the sink in my hand as I was rinsing off some dishes. It was a hot day, so the window was open, and only the screen separated Figaro from me. He let out one of his ear-piercing meows at me. I was spraying a dish when he did this. I couldn't resist. You know where this is going! Figaro got a little shower through the screen and then bolted off. This was a picture of our life together.

I was reading a chapter of Proverbs every day that month. The next day was July 12, and there was a verse the Lord had me to read that day: "A righteous man regards the life of his animal" (Proverbs 12:10). God sure knows how to convict us.

One time, Figaro hadn't come home for three days, and my wife was very worried. By this time, I was walking in a faith where I prayed like a believer should pray. I'd come to believe that God listens to our prayers, and I knew God could help us. So I told Mary I'd pray for her cat. I prayed under my breath, "Lord, you know I don't like that cat, but I love my wife. Would You please help her cat find his way home?" Five minutes later, I heard the cat's annoying meow at the front door.

I'm never surprised by answered prayers, but always amazed.

The sign of a maturing saint is that they're no longer surprised when their prayers are answered. "So we fasted and earnestly prayed that our God would take care of us, and he heard our prayer" (Ezra 8:23 NLT).

A few years later, my wife came to me and was very worried about her cat. She said he was all bloated, not moving and not eating, and he looked terrible. That was a Friday night, and the next day I had a full day of teaching at a local prison. I told her to take him to the vet the next morning—maybe the cat had worms or something. Then I would check back with her later after my day of prison ministry. By this time in my faith journey, I was even more believing in all that the Lord could do, as I'd been serving in a prison church where the move of God was commonplace. We need to believe higher than we do.

Jesus intends us to have a faith that takes hold of His power. "Then He called His twelve disciples together and gave them power and authority over all demons, and to cure diseases" (Luke 9:1).

That Saturday I came home and saw that my wife was very sad. I rarely see Mary as sad as this. I asked her what was wrong. She said the vet had checked Figaro, and he was really bad off. He'd possibly eaten something bad, his intestines were messed up, and he wasn't going to make it. The only chance would be maybe, with a $5,000 surgery. My first thought was, "That cat's going to die." We didn't have that kind of money to fix Figaro. Mary then said the vet told her to bring Figaro the next Monday to put him to sleep, as there wasn't anything they could do for him. They didn't want him to suffer.

If you want to believe more, you have to doubt less. "Jesus immediately stretched out his hand and lifted him up and said, 'What little faith you have! Why would you let doubt win?'" (Matthew 14:31 TPT).

I have this faith that just believes what Scripture says. The Lord says He can heal, so I believe He can heal. And I know that God can heal an animal just as well as He can heal a human. There's nothing He can't do. I don't know how everything works, but I know that God does a mighty work when we just ask Him in faith. I'll let other people who are smarter than me argue why it can't be done, while I just believe and then watch while it's done. We need to learn to ask the Father like a child, and to not complicate it more than just believing God can do it.

The mature believer learns to become like a little child. Jesus taught, "Whoever continually humbles himself to become like this little child is the greatest one in heaven's kingdom realm" (Matthew 18:4 TPT).

I told my wife, "Why don't we just go lay hands on your cat and pray that he'd be healed?" She thought that would be a good idea. Mary has such a simple and trusting faith. We first had dinner, as I always fasted for ministry so was very hungry. After we ate, we went out to where Figaro was lying. He looked terrible, all bloated and unable to move. I laid hands on him and started the prayer—only in my thoughts at first. "Lord, you know I don't like this cat, but I love my wife." Then I prayed out loud: "Lord, you're the God that can do anything, so I'm praying that you'd heal this cat." Friend, when I say a prayer, I believe God can do it. Can you believe?

Believe like a believer. "What do you mean, 'If I can'?" Jesus asked. 'Anything is possible if a person believes.' The father instantly cried out, 'I do believe, but help me overcome my unbelief!'" (Mark 9:23-24 NLT).

I forget what else I prayed; it was nothing special. I just pray to the Lord like I talk to people. I hear people pray to God like they're reading from a script up on a stage. I just talk the way I talk. If we don't pray real, we're fake. Where is there faith in that? I know He appreciates a genuine heart the same as we do. When you pray, don't try to sound like someone you're not, just sound like you. He made you, so I'm quite certain that's who He wants you to be.

Until you learn to pray to God with your own words, you're speaking from somebody else's heart. "When you call to me and pray to me, I will listen to you. When you seek me, you will find me, provided you seek for me wholeheartedly" (Jeremiah 29:12-13 CJB).

The next morning, we got up and were completely amazed. Figgy was running around the house as lively as a newborn kitten! He was totally healed. No bloating. No issues. All better! And that wasn't the half of it. Starting that very day, Figgy and I became friends! He started coming up to me to be petted. He wouldn't leave the room when I entered. And I don't know what happened, but from that day forward, his meow stopped bothering me. Sometimes his meow will bother my wife, but I just smile. He's my friend.

It's one thing to heal a sickness, and another to heal someone's heart.

The greatest miracle is not what God can do through you, but what God can do in you. The Lord promised, "I will put My law in their minds, and write it on their hearts; and I will be their God, and they shall be My people" (Jeremiah 31:33).

This was around ten years ago, and Figgy is now over sixteen years old. He stays inside with us all the time, not even wanting to go outside anymore. God is good. God is the God of miracles. Sometimes those good things are with grand miracles, and I've been blessed to see so many. But often, the greater miracles are in the unseen—the renewed lives, the changed hearts, and restored relationships. This is especially true between God and us. And so that the Lord could prove to me how much He can do, He didn't just heal Figgy—He made Figgy and me friends. Miracles are often never what you imagine they might be.

Stop telling God what He can't do, and just maybe He will do it. "God gives you his Spirit and works miracles in you" (Galatians 3:5 CEV).

Now it's simply inspiring to see my little buddy Figgy, and it reminds me of answered prayers, of the Lord's power to heal, not just the physical but the relational. Figaro is still a grumpy old cat and prefers Mary to anyone else. But we've remained friends to this day.

Once the Lord touches your life, you'll always remember, and your life will never be the same. Pray believing. Let God do a miracle in your life today. Ask Him to repair some broken relationship you have, and trust Him in how He will do it.

Never doubt what God can do. "The LORD answered, 'I can do anything! Watch and you'll see my words come true'" (Numbers 11:23 CEV).

Prayers

✴ *Heavenly Father, I'm Your child—help me to more fully realize that. Help me have a childlike faith, one that simply looks to You and takes You at Your Word.*

✴ *Lord Jesus, I'm Your friend, and I can speak to You just as I am. Help me to speak from my heart and to trust You more and more with every prayer I say.*

✴ *Holy Spirit, pour into me a greater anointing so that I have Your guidance and Your presence wherever I go. Help me be teachable to all that You're teaching me.*

Spiritual Growth

✴ **Treat others nicely:** We are relational creatures. Whether it be with the animals around us or the people we cross paths with each day, we need to try and have peace with everyone we encounter. We can't make someone treat us right, but we can learn to treat them right nonetheless. *Don't let how you treat others be dependent on how they treat you.* "Don't repay evil for evil. Don't snap back at those who say unkind things about you. Instead, pray for God's help for them, for we are to be kind to others, and God will bless us for it" (1 Peter 3:9 TLB).

- **Trust God:** Learning to trust the Father like His child is one of the greatest accomplishments you can have in your faith journey. This is not a fact to learn nor a skill to be trained in, but a simple act of your heart before Him. Trusting Him is by faith, and faith is in believing, and believing is the path to receiving. *Stop being so grown up in your faith that you can't believe in the power of God.* Jesus taught, "I promise you that you cannot get into God's kingdom, unless you accept it the way a child does" (Mark 10:15 CEV).

- **Learn your lesson:** Your circumstances are meant to grow you, not to destroy you. Seek the lesson your heavenly Father has for you in everything going on around you. Pray for your eyes to be opened to the spiritual truths that only the Holy Spirit can show you. *You wouldn't learn the lesson if He gave you the answers before the test was over. It's the testing in the wilderness that prepares you for the promise at the end.* It's the Lord Himself "who fed you in the wilderness...that He might humble you and that He might test you, to do you good in the end" (Deuteronomy 8:16).

9

Saved by God

Have faith that God can save you through a thing, and trust Him with whatever He does.

The three young men about to be executed by the king said this to him: "Our God whom we serve is able to deliver us from the burning fiery furnace, and He will deliver us from your hand, O king. But if not, let it be known to you, O king, that we do not serve your gods" (Daniel 3:17-18).

IF YOU CAN BELIEVE the Lord can save you, you won't worry about all the things that come against you.

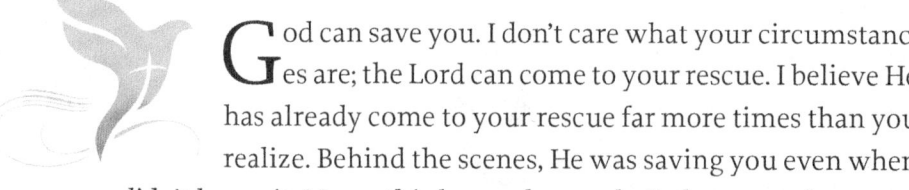

God can save you. I don't care what your circumstances are; the Lord can come to your rescue. I believe He has already come to your rescue far more times than you realize. Behind the scenes, He was saving you even when you didn't know it. Never think your heavenly Father started protecting you only after you were saved. Your Father loved you before you loved Him. You can't even imagine a love as great as His.

God loved you even when you were His enemy, and He still loves you even in your failures. "God demonstrates His own love toward us, in that while we were still sinners, Christ died for us" (Romans 5:8).

Someday we'll get to heaven and learn more about all that the Lord did for us while we were here on earth. Once we know, we'll be overwhelmed with joy and filled with adoration for Him. Your Father is so intimately acquainted with every detail of your life. Not only has He numbered the hairs on your head, but He has kept watch over every one of them. He has you perfectly in His care. I believe He will show us how He was at work in our lives from before we were born all the way until the day we took our last breath on earth.

There are two breaths of a person that are the most precious—their first and their last. We don't appreciate the value of a breath until we reach the last one. "The Spirit of God has made me, and the breath of the Almighty gives me life" (Job 33:4).

God has saved you from a thousand things, so don't focus only on the hardships you still had to go through. Those hard things you endured were for a reason, and in heaven you'll learn the full revelation of God's plan unfolded, and what He was accomplishing in your life. Your Father loves you even though it sometimes seems like He doesn't. The test of your faith is not when things are going right, but when they're going wrong. Thank Him for the good times, trust Him in the bad, and know that He's always with you.

Cherish the good memories, learn from the bad, and know that the Lord goes before you. "For you shall not go out with haste, nor go by flight;

for the LORD will go before you, and the God of Israel will be your rear guard" (Isaiah 52:12).

We may not know all the things the Lord has done for us until we get to heaven, but we should thank Him for all He has done whether or not we know them all. A thankful heart is a blessed heart, because its focus remains squarely on the goodness of God. You've no idea of all the ways the Lord has helped you, so thank Him for what you know, and thank Him in advance for what you don't know. Your Father watches over you every moment and never leaves you all alone.

Thank God in advance based on all He's done for you in the past. "LORD, I will worship you with extended hands as my whole heart explodes with praise! I will tell everyone everywhere about your wonderful works and how your marvelous miracles exceed expectations!" (Psalm 9:1 TPT).

For many years I was blessed to serve at the state prison called California Rehabilitation Center near my home. Every Saturday, I drove out early in the morning to open the chapel before the inmates were released for the program that stretched into the afternoon. One Saturday morning, I was driving along on the freeway on my way there. I was approaching an interchange to get onto another freeway. Traffic was light, since it was still early on a Saturday. I changed lanes to the right to go up this interchange as I'd done a hundred times before. Right then, in the corner of my eye, I noticed a minivan quickly cutting over several lanes to get onto the same interchange. They crossed over some distance out in front of me.

The minivan didn't make it over in time. Right in front of me, it plowed into the barrels that sit in front of the dividing wall between the freeway and the onramp. The barrels were crushed, and the whole backend of the Minivan lifted high and to the right, directly in the path of where I was headed. I was traveling very fast and had no time to react. I saw it all like it was happening in slow motion. It's often when we get near to death that we see how precious life is.

Your life matters because God says so. "How precious also are Your thoughts to me, O God! How great is the sum of them! If I should count them, they would be more in number than the sand" (Psalm 139:17-18).

Before I could do anything, something miraculous happened right before my eyes. I saw this minivan lifted and shifted over to the right by several feet. The barrels returned to how they were, and the van sped away as if nothing had ever happened.

I was blown away by what I'd witnessed. I rubbed my eyes, wondering, "Did I really just see that? Did that really just happen?" I did just see it. It did just happen.

Friend, I want you to know that we serve a God who is able to save us. "Our God is a God who saves! The Sovereign Lord rescues us from death" (Psalm 68:20 NLT).

The Lord doesn't always save us here on earth. Nobody gets off this planet alive. Eventually, He'll bring us home to heaven. The decision is always based on His plan, never on our merits. But know this: When He calls us home, nobody ever asks to return. "For to me, to live is Christ, and to die is gain" (Philippians 1:21).

Rarely do we get to see all that's in the spiritual realm around us. We see less so that we can have more faith. It's the unseen that builds up our faith the most. But on occasion, the Lord will allow our eyes to be opened so we see some of what He's doing on our behalf. It's as if the Lord pulls back the curtains for a moment so we can see what's going on behind the scenes. But rest assured, whether we see it or not, know that there's always much going on behind the scenes.

Our problem is that we believe only as far as we can see. "We don't look for things that can be seen but for things that can't be seen. Things that can be seen are only temporary. But things that can't be seen last forever" (2 Corinthians 4:18 NOG).

On that Saturday morning, it was as if the arm of the Lord reached down from heaven and picked up and shifted that minivan so the accident was avoided. Never think that the arm of the Lord is unable to reach down and save you from whatever circumstance you're in. "And the Lord said to Moses, 'Has the Lord's arm been shortened? Now you shall see whether what I say will happen to you or not'" (Numbers 11:23). Friend, I want you to know, to this day His arm has not been shortened.

I don't know the theology around how this minivan was moved, but I can tell you the Lord intervened for me on that Saturday morning. We need to increase the limit of our faith to reach into the unlimited resources of heaven. We need to believe for more, knowing that there's so much more—because our God is a God with no limits. Stir up your faith and renew your mind that you might believe in all that God can do in your life.

We think a miracle will produce faith, but it's faith that produces miracles. A jar can hold only up to its limit. By this same principle, your faith determines the degree of power that God will pour into you. "Jesus replied, 'Why do you say "if you can"? Anything is possible for someone who has faith!'" (Mark 9:23 CEV).

I want you to know, the Lord has saved you a hundred times over, and you had no idea. You, too, have been saved by the grace of God. Learn to praise Him in the good times and the bad, knowing that He's doing a work in your life through every circumstance. Trust in the Lord despite all you see in the natural, knowing that there's so much more the Lord is doing for you behind the scenes. Trust the Lover of your eternal soul.

Never let the limit of your sight be the limit of your faith. "Elisha prayed, and said, 'Lord, I pray, open his eyes that he may see.' Then the Lord opened the eyes of the young man, and he saw. And behold, the mountain was full of horses and chariots of fire all around Elisha" (2 Kings 6:17).

Perhaps you're already aware of a time when the Lord saved you. It was such a miracle that there are no natural explanations possible.

God saved you for a reason. There is yet something more that He has for you to do. And even if you're not aware of being saved by God, know this: If you're breathing, He has a reason for your being still alive. Serve God with all your heart, and know that He has you every step of the way.

Father God loves you unconditionally and Jesus saved you unequivocally. Now be the son or daughter of the King that you were meant to be. "The Lord Almighty says, 'I will be your Father, and you will be my sons and daughters'" (2 Corinthians 6:18 NOG).

Prayers

* *Heavenly Father, thank You for saving me from the dangers in this world. Thank You for those things You saved me from, whether I knew of them or not.*

* *Lord Jesus, thank You for saving me for all eternity, that by Your sacrifice on the cross, through Your blood alone, I can live forever in heaven with You.*

* *Holy Spirit, open my eyes so I learn more of what the Father is doing for me here on earth, so I will forever praise His name on earth and in heaven.*

Spiritual Growth

* **Believe that God loves you:** Learn to believe in God's unfailing love toward you. The more you know you're loved, the less vulnerable you'll be. Stop thinking His love depends on your works, but declare the truth as found in His Word that His love endures forever. *Jesus loves you. You can't change Him loving you, but you'll*

change as you love Him. "Through the Lord's mercies we are not consumed, because His compassions fail not. They are new every morning; great is Your faithfulness" (Lamentations 3:22-23).

- **Believe that God is with you:** There's nothing you need fear and nothing you need dread as long as you know that the Lord is at your side. Trust in His promises as given in His Holy Word. *In whatever you're going through, He has you.* "Do not be afraid or discouraged, for the Lord will personally go ahead of you. He will be with you; he will neither fail you nor abandon you" (Deuteronomy 31:8 NLT).

- **Believe that God can save you:** No matter your circumstances or what people are saying around you, trust that God can save you. *When people say you don't have a prayer, simply fall to your knees and prove them wrong. "Impossible" is a word found only in the vocabulary of the unbeliever.* "And you know in all your hearts and in all your souls that not one thing has failed of all the good things which the Lord your God spoke concerning you. All have come to pass for you; not one word of them has failed" (Joshua 23:14).

10

Classroom of Adversity

Your life is the classroom, and your circumstances are the lesson.

"For you know that when your faith is tested it stirs up power within you to endure all things" (James 1:3 TPT).

IF YOU CAN BELIEVE that the Father has only your best eternal interests in mind, you'll trust Him in the midst of your trials.

Adversity is a harsh teacher that seldom lets us off the hook without first giving us a hard lesson. One lesson that's especially hard is in knowing that God can do all things even when He chooses not to. Our faith is tested the most in adversity because it's in adversity that we must learn to trust a God who lets us suffer. There's no lesson harder than to be placed where we think God Himself has forsaken us.

Sometimes God makes it seem as if He has forsaken you so you'll discover that He never will. "The LORD is good, a stronghold in the day of trouble; and He knows those who trust in Him" (Nahum 1:7).

If we want to believe with a higher faith, we must have our faith tested so that it might grow. It's easy to believe when things are going well, when it seems as though the Lord is answering your every prayer. But the good times don't build your faith. It's when things are going terribly wrong, when it's as if God isn't even listening to you, that your faith is stretched to the limit.

When God is silent, He's teaching you to trust Him. "Trust in Him at all times, you people; pour out your heart before Him; God is a refuge for us. Selah" (Psalm 62:8).

Nobody prays for a trial, and we don't have to, because they come without asking for them. It's in the fiery furnace of tribulation where many will turn away from the faith, proving that their faith wasn't rooted properly to begin with. But others will be tested and their faith found true, and this faith is strengthened in the midst of their trials. Suffering proves what's really at the foundation of our faith. We must walk in the wilderness to see what's in our heart.

If you didn't have the trials, you wouldn't know what you were made of. "And you shall remember that the LORD your God led you all the way these forty years in the wilderness, to humble you and test you, to know what was in your heart, whether you would keep His commandments or not" (Deuteronomy 8:2).

I don't know all that you've been through in your life, but I know you've suffered. Everyone suffers. The question for us all is how we suffer. Either we trust in God to get us through it, or we become angry at Him for allowing it. We often start out in our anger, and over time the Lord will show us the way to trust Him. Learning to trust Him in adversity gives us the strength we need to get through it. And once we're through it, the faith He has formed in us prepares us for all that lies ahead.

Never squander that which only adversity can produce in your life. "Though the Lord gave you adversity for food and suffering for drink, he will still be with you to teach you. You will see your teacher with your own eyes. Your own ears will hear him. Right behind you a voice will say, 'This is the way you should go,' whether to the right or to the left" (Isaiah 30:20-21 NLT).

Many years ago, I went to a ministry event at a men's prison that lasted the whole day. We'd brought in musicians, praise dancers, and various guests to speak to the men throughout the day. The event was held in a chapel that held around three hundred men. The chapel had a large raised stage up front so that everyone could see who was speaking or performing. It's such a blessing for me to see the many saints who pour out so much as they serve the kingdom of God. The ones who impress me most are the ones who aren't trying to impress me.

The lack of kingdom work is not because Christians won't do the big things, but because they won't do the small things. Jesus taught, "If anyone desires to be first, he shall be last of all and servant of all" (Mark 9:35).

In the middle of the program, I was given a few minutes to speak, so I gave a short testimony. I consider a testimony to be especially effective because you aren't arguing to someone what they should do, but you're only baring your soul in what the Lord Jesus has done for you. Your testimony shows others where you were before Christ and where you are now after He has changed your life. If we want to convince others about how Jesus can change lives, we must have a life in which we can show it.

The most powerful message you can preach is your testimony. After Jesus delivered a man from demons, He told him, "Go home to your friends, and tell them what great things the Lord has done for you, and how He has had compassion on you" (Mark 5:19).

As I often do, I started my testimony with how a teenage boy tried to kill me when I was fifteen. He snuck up behind me and started to choke me. I wasn't startled and didn't try to get away. Instead, I just relaxed and welcomed the chance to end my misery. For my entire life, I've had so much pain every day because my senses are broken. By the time I was fifteen, I'd had enough of the pain. I wasn't afraid to die; I was afraid of all the pain that I would have to endure if I remained living.

As a diamond is formed in adversity, so it is that the Lord allows His servants to be formed. "We also glory in tribulations, knowing that tribulation produces perseverance; and perseverance, character" (Romans 5:3-4).

Clearly, I didn't die on that day. I came to after passing out, and that boy was gone. I never saw him again. I still remember the look in his eyes. Now, since I've grown in my faith, I know that look, and this boy had demons living within him. On that day the Lord intervened and didn't allow that boy to kill me. It's as if God reached down from heaven and put His hand between that demon-possessed boy and me, and He said about me, "Not today—he's mine."

The Lord has His hand in our life long before we ever come to Him. It was many years after this event before I came to Christ, but I'll never forget that day. The Father saves us for a reason.

He will not take you up onto the mountain until you first learn to trust Him in the valley. "Yea, though I walk through the valley of the shadow of death, I will fear no evil: for thou art with me" (Psalm 23:4 KJV).

There are so many people struggling in our day with the trials in their life. So many have no hope, and they see no reason to keep living.

People today carry so many burdens, and they need us Christians to reach out and help them. We need to stop judging their sin and start rescuing them with love. Let us have hearts for the hurting and compassion for the lost. How we treat others matters more than you know. Be gentle with everyone. Choose to be the person bringing the light of Christ within them, and be the ray of hope someone desperately needs.

Your most powerful display of Christ in you is in your gentleness. "Be gentle to all" (2 Timothy 2:24).

As I continue with the rest of my testimony, I love to tell how the Lord rescued me from my darkness and brought me into His glorious light. I speak about how messed up I was before Christ, so that it might be an encouragement to anyone listening who's still messed up. If you want to pick someone up, you must kneel down to reach them. It's a joy to talk about how the Lord rescued me and how He can rescue all of us.

On that full day of ministry years ago in that prison, I don't know if my testimony touched anyone or not. We don't have to worry about how God will use our testimony, but only tell it. It will be your story that touches someone like nobody else can.

There are two parts to your salvation: Jesus did it all, and you can do nothing. "For by grace you have been saved through faith, and that not of yourselves; it is the gift of God, not of works, lest anyone should boast" (Ephesians 2:8-9).

Later that day, the prison chaplain asked me to escort the praise dancers out of the prison. They couldn't stay to the end of the program and needed someone to escort them to the front gate. It was a long walk, and along the way we were talking about the program. They were young ladies in their early twenties, just starting out in their faith journey. One of them asked me about my sensory condition that I shared about in my testimony. She asked me when it was that God delivered me from that condition. I told her that the Lord hadn't delivered me from it yet, but He was surely helping me through it.

Don't focus on your problems, but on the Lord who's helping you through them. "There is no one like the God of Israel. He rides across the heavens to help you, across the skies in majestic splendor" (Deuteronomy 33:26 NLT).

Some people teach that we must never accept any condition where we might suffer. They say God's will is for us to always be healthy and pain-free. These teachers are wrong. They teach a message that pleases the flesh and makes them more popular to the world. God is not in the business of making us happy, but of making us holy. Sometimes the Lord chooses to leave us in a painful or undesirable condition, and we must learn to trust Him with His decision. God does His greatest work during the worst times of your life. Never despise the suffering that brings about the purposes of God in your life.

Don't be bitter about the trial that God is using to shape you. "Therefore, as the Holy Spirit says: 'Today, if you will hear His voice, do not harden your hearts as in the rebellion, in the day of trial in the wilderness'" (Hebrews 3:7-8). *Let your wilderness grow you.*

We can always pray for healing. As long as a person has breath, I pray for their healing here on earth. We can pray believing for a miracle because God is able to do a miracle. But friend, the Lord sometimes chooses not to do miracles. We must still believe in all He can do whether He does it or not. Sometimes it's the suffering that brings the real healing that the Lord is looking for. It takes a special level of faith to trust Him during times of intense suffering. It will be these times that your faith will grow the most.

Trusting is highest when your understanding is lowest. "Preserve me, O God, for in You I put my trust" (Psalm 16:1).

I once had a vision in which I saw Jesus. This is a rare event for me; it has happened only a few times. I was given the chance to ask Him one question, any question I wanted. I asked Him the question many of us would: Why? I wanted to know why He'd allowed me to suffer so much in my life. Before I understood my condition, I grew up thinking people were hurting me on purpose. Later I lived in shame because people couldn't understand my condition, because it's so different. Not only did I have to suffer, but I had to suffer alone while being misunderstood. I lived in pain, trying to live a normal life, but never being able to. So that was my question: Why? I think most people would ask the same question for whatever suffering they're going through.

Pray that your suffering accomplishes His will for your life. "May the God of all grace, who called us to His eternal glory by Christ Jesus, after you have suffered a while, perfect, establish, strengthen, and settle you" (1 Peter 5:10).

I was holding His hands in this vision as I asked Him this question. I was looking into His eyes and waiting for Him to answer me. All He said was this: *"To draw you closer to Myself."* This had a great impact on me. I felt a flood of bad memories being released with the purpose revealed in my suffering. We don't always get to know the reason we suffer, but we can always trust in Him through all that we're going through. God never squanders that which was paid for with suffering.

Jesus loves you so much that there's no suffering He would withhold from you if it draws you nearer to Himself. "These little troubles are getting us ready for an eternal glory that will make all our troubles seem like nothing" (2 Corinthians 4:17 CEV).

Perhaps you need to ask Jesus why He has let you suffer. Be willing to listen for what He might say. If we're to endure all that we'll go through, we must learn to believe that God can help us, God can comfort us, and He can deliver us from whatever it is we're up against. But we must also have the faith and believe in His power even when He chooses not to use it. Learn to believe more than you complain, and your life will be a blessing for the kingdom.

Sometimes suffering is meant to be your platform to help others see how to get through a similar trial in their life. Trust Him in your suffering.

Jesus had faith that His Father could save Him from suffering. He also had faith that His Father would help Him through it. Jesus prayed just before His crucifixion, "O My Father, if it is possible, let this cup pass from Me; nevertheless, not as I will, but as You will" (Matthew 26:39).

Prayers

* *Heavenly Father, help me better realize that no matter how difficult my circumstances, You're there with me and can use everything to work out Your purposes through me.*

* *Lord Jesus, teach me to know by the example of Your life how God transforms what we think is a tragedy into His eternal plans and purposes here on earth.*

* *Holy Spirit, teach me to realize the power of believing through adversity, and help me in that process. Help me grow in my faith through the difficult circumstances in my life.*

Spiritual Growth

* **Remember lessons learned:** Reflect back on trials you've been through, in which the Lord has done a work in your life. Consider how He has formed you in adversity for a purpose and prepared you for all eternity. Write out how He has helped you through adversity. *There's no such thing as a self-made man or woman in the kingdom of God.* "And the vessel that he made of clay was marred in the hand of the potter; so he made it again into another vessel, as it seemed good to the potter to make" (Jeremiah 18:4).

* **Let go of the past:** Don't allow what has gone wrong in your life to ruin you. Only the devil wants you to be ruined, whereas God is

using everything for the good of those who love Him. Rebuke out loud any root of bitterness you're holding onto. *Circumstances don't define who we are—they reveal who we are.* "You have been grieved by various trials, that the genuineness of your faith...though it is tested by fire, may be found to praise, honor, and glory at the revelation of Jesus Christ" (1 Peter 1:6-7).

- **Press ahead:** Start developing a kingdom mindset. Consider all you've been through and all you're going through now, and determine to believe that through every trial, God will form you and use you for His kingdom. Pray that the Holy Spirit will reveal this to you. *Don't let your past be an anchor, but a stepping-stone.* "One thing I do, forgetting those things which are behind and reaching forward to those things which are ahead, I press toward the goal for the prize of the upward call of God in Christ Jesus" (Philippians 3:13-14).

11

God's Provisions

God created everything from nothing, and He can meet your needs in the same way.

"I lift up my eyes to the hills. From where does my help come? My help comes from the Lord, who made heaven and earth" (Psalm 121:1-2 ESV).

IF YOU CAN BELIEVE the Lord can meet your every need, you'll stop worrying so much about your job and your finances.

One area that often tests our belief is the things we're in need of. We live in a world of scarcity, and it seems we're often a heartbeat away from losing everything. We're always lacking something. It's in this state of need where God tests our faith and asks us to trust in Him with all that we need. The resources in heaven are never scarce, and God can give us more than we ever need. Yet He chooses not to, and instead uses our needs to develop our faith in all that He can provide. The thing you need most turns you to the Lord the most.

We pray the most in the hardest of times—that's why the Lord allows them. "In my distress I called upon the Lord, and cried out to my God; He heard my voice from His temple, and my cry came before Him, even to His ears" (Psalm 18:6).

Provisions aren't only finances, but include whatever thing you're in need of. It may be the courage to overcome an obstacle. It could be the wisdom to make a right decision. It can be a material thing like transportation. It can be a physical need, like the strength to endure a long work shift. Whatever it is you need, you can turn to the Lord for the provision. I'm always surprised with the imagination of the Lord in how He helps me.

Child of God, ask your Father for what you need and believe that He can do it.

The most productive time in your day is when you're sitting in prayer before the Lord. "I, Lord, have cried out to You for help, and in the morning my prayer comes before You" (Psalm 88:13 NASB).

One provision I'm always finding myself pleading to the Lord for is the help I need in order to serve Him rightly. I've always had such a deep sense of inadequacy. Certainly in ministry there are always people far more qualified than I am. I have neither the charm nor the intellect to impress anyone. But I have Jesus, and He's enough. I want you to know that in whatever it is you're lacking, He is always enough.

Whatever your need, it's there to build up your faith in what He can do. Believe for more—that the more would be coming.

Believe for more, then pray for more—that the will of God will be done on earth. Jesus taught us to pray for God's will: "In this manner, therefore, pray: '...Your will be done on earth as it is in heaven'" (Matthew 6:9-10).

I'm not the smartest believer. I just believe what the Word says. I'm not educated enough or smart enough to argue away the power of God. I pray that you're not that smart either. It's with a childlike faith that we can rest in the perfect care of our heavenly Father. When a child needs something from their father, they simply ask him and believe that he'll take care of them. Child of God, do the same with your heavenly Father. Go to Him with a childlike faith, and simply tell Him what you need. Then believe that He'll take care of you.

Learn to believe like a little child. The problem in our churches is that we have too many who believe like adults. Jesus taught, "Whoever does not receive the kingdom of God [with faith and humility] like a child will not enter it at all" (Luke 18:17 AMP).

For several years I was blessed to preach and teach at different prisons. To reach these prisons from my house, I traveled around thirty miles through some of the worst freeways on this planet. One time I left my house to go out and lead a program at a prison. I don't even remember what the program was on that day, but I do remember getting into my wife's old car to drive out there. Normally on the day and time I left, the freeways would be wide open, and I'd get there in good time. Still, I always left home early and arrived there early. Our promptness for a thing reveals our commitment to it. It baffles me that everyone can get to the theater on time but is always late for church.

How you steward time reflects your attitude toward the One who has given it to you. "So teach us to number our days, that we may apply our hearts unto wisdom" (Psalm 90:12 KJV).

I drove through the streets and got onto the freeway, and started heading toward the prison. I didn't get very far when traffic came to a stop. It started to crawl and was going very slow. It was then that I looked down and noticed the gas gauge was showing below empty. I was several miles from an exit, and this old car of my wife's was really bad about using a lot of gas. At the rate I was moving, I knew I'd end up running out of gas and missing the program at the prison.

Every circumstance is a chance to check your faith and see how much you really believe.

Circumstances don't reveal how big God is, but how big your faith is. "I am the Lord, the God of all mankind. Is anything too hard for me?" (Jeremiah 32:27 NIV).

There I was, stuck on the freeway, running late to the program, out of gas, and nowhere near an offramp or a gas station. I immediately went into prayer, asking the Lord to help me. Often when I need His help, I don't know exactly how He might help me. I don't have to worry about that part. All I have to do is pray to the Lord and tell Him what I need. Scripture tells us to make our requests known to Him, not to tell Him how to fulfill the requests. So that's what I do. I just tell Him what I need and believe that He can help me.

Give the Lord your worries, and He'll give you His peace. Stop negotiating for a better deal, for there's none better than this. "Don't worry about anything, but pray about everything. With thankful hearts offer up your prayers and requests to God. Then, because you belong to Christ Jesus, God will bless you with peace that no one can completely understand. And this peace will control the way you think and feel" (Philippians 4:6-7 CEV).

I was praying as I was crawling along that freeway, and I thanked Him for all that He does for me. I've learned to put my focus on what He's done for me in the past and not on what didn't happen. I trust Him when He doesn't answer a prayer in the way I'd wanted Him to. I trust Him to answer a prayer only when the prayer is in His will. I don't have to add "if it's in your will" to my prayers because I already know that's how He'll always answer. It's not like He might accidentally do something outside His will if we forget to remind Him! Just tell Him what you need, and trust Him with His answer.

We don't have to have all the answers—but only trust that the Lord does. "How great is our God! There's absolutely nothing his power cannot accomplish, and he has infinite understanding of everything" (Psalm 147:5 TPT).

I kept pressing in with prayer. We need to learn to pray like we mean it. We need to pray like believers. I wanted to serve God mightily in the prison, and if I was going to teach on the power of a God who can do anything, I'd have to pray as if I believe it. I'm convinced that messages spoken apart from faith have little or no power in them. If we want to set an example as a believer, we must believe.

The measure you compel others about Jesus is the measure that you live what you say. Only say what you live. Never preach lies. "Be an example to all believers in what you say, in the way you live, in your love, your faith, and your purity" (1 Timothy 4:12 NLT).

As I was praying out loud, I looked down and noticed something very unusual. I was looking at the gas gauge to see if it was slipping down even further, when I noticed it was actually slipping upward. I couldn't believe my eyes! The fuel limit was increasing. It passed the empty mark and started filling up more and more. It was growing slowly but surely as I watched. It made it all the way to a quarter tank of gas. I was praising God for His provision!

A thankful heart knows and trusts that the Lord is good. "Oh, give thanks to the LORD, for He is good! For His mercy endures forever" (Psalm 136:1).

The traffic eventually cleared, and the car had fuel to spare, so I made it to the prison on time. I don't remember the lesson I gave that day in prison, but I can assure you I remember the lesson I learned on the way there.

Friend, our heavenly Father can provide for us beyond what we can imagine. *Pray to His limits, not yours.* I remember thinking that day, "I should've prayed for a full tank of gas!" Let's not get so serious in our life that we forget to smile. God is surely smiling down on us.

If you just smiled more, you would frown less. Let the power of joy rule in your life! "You will show me the path of life; in Your presence is fullness of joy; at Your right hand are pleasures forevermore" (Psalm 16:11).

This was a little miracle, but it had a big impact on my life. When the Lord answers a prayer, never try to explain it away as if He wasn't the one who helped you. I knew that God had helped me that day. It was a small thing, but the Lord is as interested in the small things as the big things. Sometimes He tests us in the little to see what we might do with the much. Before we pray for anything, we must ask: "Do I believe God can help?" We tend to pray to the limit that we believe. Believe for more, and let God be God.

You can't take hold of the promises of God while firmly holding onto the doubts of your mind. "Because of their unbelief, he couldn't do any miracles among them except to place his hands on a few sick people and heal them" (Mark 6:5 NLT).

Prayers

* *Heavenly Father, I know that You love me so perfectly and completely. You can take care of my every need, and all I must do is ask You. Help me, Lord, with all my needs.*

* *Lord Jesus, You stepped into time to save me. And if I can trust in You for my eternal salvation, then most certainly I can trust You for the needs in this day.*

* *Holy Spirit, guide me to discern between things I need and things that stand between my Father and me. Help me to seek only what glorifies Christ Jesus in my life.*

Spiritual Growth

- **Seek God first:** Seek the Lord more than you seek the things you want Him to give you. When we seek Him in this way, it reflects our trust that He'll take care of us without our even needing to ask Him. *It's not that you're seeking wrong things, but that you're seeking them in the wrong order.* The Lord Jesus instructed us, "Seek first the kingdom of God and His righteousness, and all these things [your earthly needs] shall be added to you" (Matthew 6:33).

- **Never give up:** Never give up in your prayers. Never give in to your worries. Keep the faith and trust the Lord with everything you take to Him. *Never give up on God, because God will never give up on you.* "Yahweh is the one who is going ahead of you. He will be with you. He won't abandon you or leave you. So don't be afraid or terrified" (Deuteronomy 31:8 NOG).

- **Remember His faithfulness:** Keep track of all the ways the Lord has provided for you. Write them out. Read them aloud. Whenever you're facing a great need, go back to this list and praise the Lord for all He has done for you in your life. *You'll never be lacking when once you're drawing from the resources of heaven. Never allow the limits of man to be the high mark of your life.* "The young lions lack and suffer hunger; but those who seek the Lord shall not lack any good thing" (Psalm 34:10).

12

Pray the Promise

The Word of God is the promise of God.

"For though a thousand generations may pass away, he is still true to his word. He has kept every promise" (Psalm 105:8-9 TPT).

IF YOU CAN BELIEVE that the Word is the promise of God, you'll take hold of the promises He has for you.

The Word of God contains the promises of God, which were given to us that we might believe them. When we read a promise and believe it, power can be found. You have to believe the promises before you can stand on them. This doesn't mean we can distort the Word into a false promise and expect to receive it. But what it does mean is that we can trust that the actual promises of God found in the Word are true and never changing. The promises of God are the power He has given to those willing to believe Him.

Pray like a believer. Jesus promised, "And whatever you ask in My name, that I will do, that the Father may be glorified in the Son. If you ask anything in My name, I will do it" (John 14:13-14).

A practice I began many years ago is to pray the promises of God, so that He hears them coming back to Himself from me. I remind my Father of what He promised in His Word. It's not that my Father would forget His Word, but I want Him to know what I'm standing on. I don't always know what words of my own I should pray, but I know that when I pray His promises I'm praying on the foundation of His power and His truth that will stand forever. When we pray the Word, we pray the promise.

We can't always rely upon the good intentions of man, but only on the promises of God. People will often fail you, but the Lord never will. The Lord promises us, "Don't be afraid, for I am with you. Don't be discouraged, for I am your God. I will strengthen you and help you. I will hold you up with my victorious right hand" (Isaiah 41:10 NLT).

Several years ago, I was working in a career that I'd been in for my whole life. I'd started in that industry as a young teenager, and I was hoping to stay in it my entire life. I was happy with what I was doing. My work place was a reasonable distance from my house and wasn't too far from the prisons where I'd go minister after work. It seemed that God had arranged a wonderful situation for me. The good seasons are always such a blessing, and we must cherish them. Yet we must realize that the seasons are always changing.

As the seasons change, so must you. "For everything there is a season, a time for every activity under heaven" (Ecclesiastes 3:1 NLT).

One day, the CEO of my company called us all together and let us know that we'd been bought by a larger company. With my position I knew what this meant—that my job would soon be over. By this time, the industry I was in had almost entirely gone overseas, so there were few opportunities for me to stay in my career.

By the humor of heaven, that very night I was starting to teach a twelve-week class at the local state prison for women, and the subject for the class was on how to get a job. Often the Lord has us go through something so we can help others going through the very same thing. God's timing is perfect.

Nothing happens by chance or by accident with our Sovereign Lord. "For of Him and through Him and to Him are all things, to whom be glory forever. Amen" (Romans 11:36).

The class I was teaching took on a far greater meaning, given my circumstances. I'd taught this same class at the men's prison several times, so I knew the material well. But until you live a thing, you can't really teach it. I think God will often place those obstacles in our life so we can learn how to help other people overcome them. Don't despise the lesson God is teaching you. Know that God is for you and can use everything for His kingdom. We don't have to know His plan to trust Him with it. Believe that He's doing something for you, even if it seems He isn't.

We must keep our faith focused on the unseen, even when the seen is staring us right in the face. "For our light affliction, which is but for a moment, is working for us a far more exceeding and eternal weight of glory, while we do not look at the things which are seen, but at the things which are not seen. For the things which are seen are temporary, but the things which are not seen are eternal" (2 Corinthians 4:17-18).

I began my job search in full gear, using all the techniques that I'd been teaching. I'd been in this one industry for my whole life, with most of it at this one company, so I felt very unsure about getting a new job. It was during this time that I chose a banner verse to carry in this season. A banner verse is one from God's Word that you choose to be the banner of hope over your life. We should all have a banner verse over our life for the season we're in. At this time, my banner verse was—"Be strong and of good courage; do not be afraid, nor be dismayed, for the LORD your God is with you wherever you go" (Joshua 1:9).

I started sending out resumes in response to every opening I learned about that was anywhere within driving range of the prisons where I was doing ministry. My prayer was to find a job close enough to the prisons to stay in ministry. My other prayer was to find a job before this new company would show me the door. This went on for several months, and I never received one phone call or email response to all my inquiries. I wasn't sure why my Father wasn't providing for me. Didn't He want me to remain in ministry? I expanded my search much farther to where I'd have had to abandon prison ministry. Still, nobody ever contacted me.

Nobody appreciates the mountaintop as much as those who've endured the valley.

Mountaintops inspire, but it's in the valleys below where a saint is shaped for the real work of God. Never imagine an easy Christian life, but never doubt that the Lord will always be with you. "Yes, though I walk through the [deep, sunless] valley of the shadow of death, I will fear or dread no evil, for You are with me; Your rod [to protect] and Your staff [to guide], they comfort me" (Psalm 23:4 AMPC).

I was becoming fearful. I was worried that I might not be able to get a job and care for my family. I was disheartened that prison ministry might end for me. We must never be ashamed to speak about when our faith has weakened, because others need to know they're not alone. Through this time, I kept persisting in prayer. Whatever it is you're dealing with, take it to the Lord in prayer.

You have to go through the wilderness to get to the promise. Don't despise what you're going through, but know that He's with you. "For the LORD your God is living among you. He is a mighty savior. He will take delight in you with gladness. With his love, he will calm all your fears. He will rejoice over you with joyful songs" (Zephaniah 3:17 NLT).

I wrote out several verses of God's promises contained in His Word. I'd pray those promises back to the Lord, believing in every word that was written out on the pages of Holy Scripture. As we believe the Word more, we'll find our footing and not be shaken by all the things going on around us. Whenever you're frustrated or fearful, go into the Word of God and discover the peace and the power He has for you there. Nobody who goes into the Word with a trusting heart comes out the same person they were before. Trust His promises.

There are more promises in the Word than we've accepted. "For every word God speaks is sure and every promise pure. His truth is tested, found to be flawless, and ever faithful" (Psalm 12:6 TPT).

One morning I was driving to work and just praising the Lord for all that He was doing. I still hadn't found a new job, and I was losing hope that I could stay in prison ministry. But I knew and trusted that no matter my situation, God is good. I was praying as I was driving and told the Lord, "Wouldn't it be cool if You got me a job right in the middle of the three prisons I serve in?" While I was driving to work that morning and praying, a man from my church sent me an email with a job opening he'd received from an acquaintance. A few minutes later, I got to work and checked my email where I found that email at the top of my inbox. The job described fit my skills perfectly. And the job was located right in the middle of the three prisons I served in!

We need to believe that God can do the impossible.

When you can stand on the Word of God, you're able to reach into the resources of heaven. Your ministry is limited not by what you have, but by what you believe. "Then Peter said [to the lame man begging for money], 'Silver and gold I do not have, but what I do have I give you: In the name of Jesus Christ of Nazareth, rise up and walk.' And he took him by the right hand and lifted him up, and immediately his feet and ankle bones received strength" (Acts 3:6-7).

I was praying as I went to interview for this new job. I had such confidence—not in myself, but in my God, who was the power that went before me. I remember thinking that there was hardly a need to interview me, since the Lord had already given me this job. They did hire me, and I went on to do ministry in the prisons for many more years. And even better, since I was so close to the prisons with this new job, I was able to increase the ministry, going in more days each week. It's one thing to know the Word of God and another to believe it.

Pray the promise and let God answer as He will.

When finally you believe the Word, nothing will seem impossible to you. "For with God nothing will be impossible" (Luke 1:37).

In my family, miracles are commonplace. We see God acting in so many ways with such incredible faithfulness that we're hardly surprised by all that He's doing. Yet when He does a thing, we thank Him for it and praise Him for being true to His promises.

Perhaps you, too, have seen the promises in His Word become realized in your life. Thank Him for that. And if you've not yet walked believing in His promises, then determine in your heart that this will change today. Go find your banner verse for the season you're in now, and let that verse come alive in you.

Faith is not the lack of obstacles, but trusting in Him to get you through them. "You are of God, little children, and have overcome them, because He who is in you is greater than he who is in the world" (1 John 4:4).

Prayers

✴ *Heavenly Father, thank You for all the promises You've made to me in Your Word. Help me hold on tightly to these promises as I go through the storms in my life.*

✴ *Lord Jesus, I love the way You spoke the words of Scripture, expressing them as simple and powerful truths from God. Help me to more fully receive these promises in the Word.*

✴ *Holy Spirit, bring to my remembrance the words of Christ, so that I would live them. Help me have a faith that believes upon every promise spoken in Holy Scripture.*

Spiritual Growth

✴ **Choose a banner verse:** Select one promise of God as written in His Holy Word that speaks to you for the season you're in right now. Make this verse the banner over your life today. Write out this verse and place it before you in all the places you spend your time. Be ready to tell people why this promise of God means so much to you. *You'll never fall when standing on the Word of God.* "For the word of God is living and powerful" (Hebrews 4:12).

✴ **Have a real faith:** Be willing to rip down the façade of a faith that you don't yet have. As you speak to others, allow yourself to be vulnerable in whatever level of faith you have. We can help others more when they see we're just like them. Humility admits reality. *You won't be filled with humility until you first swallow your pride.* "A man's pride and sense of self-importance will bring him down, but he who has a humble spirit will obtain honor" (Proverbs 29:23 AMP).

✴ **Pray the promise:** Start to include the Word of God in your prayers. When we remind God of His promises, we're being reminded of them ourselves. Write down verses you would like to pray back to the Lord. Speak them out loud so that even the demonic realm will hear what God has promised you. *Don't focus on the troubles in this world, but on the promises born out of heaven.* The Lord Jesus taught, "These things I have spoken to you, that in Me you may have peace. In the world you will have tribulation; but be of good cheer, I have overcome the world" (John 16:33).

13

Holy Spirit

The proof of the Holy Spirit in you is the Holy Spirit through you. The waters aren't still, but flowing.

The Lord Jesus revealed, "'Have faith in me, and you will have life-giving water flowing from deep inside you, just as the Scriptures say.' Jesus was talking about the Holy Spirit, who would be given to everyone that had faith in him" (John 7:38-39 CEV).

IF YOU CAN BELIEVE the Holy Spirit dwells within you, you'll have no doubts that He can talk to you and lead you on what to do.

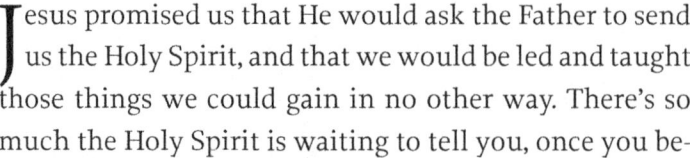

Jesus promised us that He would ask the Father to send us the Holy Spirit, and that we would be led and taught those things we could gain in no other way. There's so much the Holy Spirit is waiting to tell you, once you believe and then listen for Him. There are levels you can get to in your faith by no other way but to have the Spirit of God whispering into your heart. The Holy Spirit is able to do the impossible, even with changing you. Don't squander the gift that God has for you.

The Holy Spirit is not a prize to win but a gift to receive. "Peter replied, 'Each of you must repent of your sins and turn to God, and be baptized in the name of Jesus Christ for the forgiveness of your sins. Then you will receive the gift of the Holy Spirit.'" (Acts 2:38 NLT).

The Holy Spirit was sent to help us in our faith journey. He can guide us in every decision we have. He can teach us things about the Word of God and how it relates to everything around us. The Holy Spirit can bring you revelations that can change your life.

The promise of the Holy Spirit was meant for us all. When once you've received Jesus as your Savior, then by the promises of God you can receive the Holy Spirit. And once you receive the Holy Spirit in fullness, your life will be transformed into something beautiful and new.

When you're filled by the Holy Spirit, you're no longer just a man or a woman. "Therefore do not be foolish and thoughtless, but understand and firmly grasp what the will of the Lord is.... Be filled with the [Holy] Spirit and constantly guided by Him" (Ephesians 5:17-18 AMP).

During the many years I served in prison ministry, I was so blessed by all the believers I met along the way. I was being exposed to more and more anointed believers who walked in the power of the Holy Spirit. But for many years I didn't walk in much power. We need to learn to serve as we are, knowing that our Father will give us what we need as we're serving. I'm most certain that God was still forming that new heart within me.

God will never take you up the mountain until He has first prepared you in the valley below. Never rush God because only He knows when you're ready.

Stop seeking the gifts of the Spirit while thinking you might serve God with them. Instead, serve God as you are—so that He then provides you the necessary gifts in the midst of your serving. "There are different spiritual gifts, but the same Spirit gives them. The evidence of the Spirit's presence is given to each person for the common good of everyone" (1 Corinthians 12:4,7 NOG).

After four years of ministering inside prisons, I had the wonderful experience of being baptized in the Holy Spirit. This is an experience in which the fullness of the Holy Spirit takes a far greater hold in the life of a believer. If you've not yet experienced this, make it your prayer that you would experience it. This happened to me after I'd been doing ministry in the prisons for a few days while also fasting. Then I went to a gathering, and it was there my life was changed forever. How much we need to have these life-changing experiences in our faith journey! We're meant to grow in our faith, and it's the Lord who helps us to do this.

Growing in faith is not changing yourself, but being changed. Spiritual power is not built up, but poured in. Moses said, "Oh, that all the Lord's people were prophets and that the Lord would put His Spirit upon them!" (Numbers 11:29).

About a year after being baptized in the Holy Spirit, I had another life-changing experience. One afternoon I got a phone call from my dear friend Bonnie Calkins. She'd put together an impromptu gathering for a small group at her house. She'd invited six young people whom we both knew to come over. As soon as she called me, I jumped at the chance to come over. Whenever there's a meeting at Bonnie's house, the Holy Spirit is sure to be there overflowing.

Wherever you are, find the remnant and get close to them.

Minister to the masses, but only be joined to the remnant. "In the same way then, there has also come to be at the present time a remnant according to God's gracious choice" (Romans 11:5 NASB).

When I got to Bonnie's house, she was sharing on one of her many messages. During the meeting, it became apparent to me that I wouldn't be able to stay. God has seen to it that I was born with a sensory condition that makes many situations unbearable. Usually I just spend all my time alone, so I don't have to deal with the possibility of these bad experiences. But I love to be with others, and I deeply long for times of fellowship and worship. Often I'm able to find a way to do it. But I never know when a situation will be okay for me or not. If it becomes too much, I just leave. I don't get upset, because I know the Lord still has me.

Never squander suffering knowing all that God can do through it. Joseph told his brothers, "As for you, you meant evil against me; but God meant it for good, in order to bring it about as it is this day, to save many people alive" (Genesis 50:20).

With great regret, I got up and left. I was going down the stairs outside the house when Bonnie came out and stopped me. She wanted to know if I disagreed with her teaching. Oh, no, that wasn't it! I let her know it was because of the pain that was flowing in through my senses. Bonnie knew I had this condition. We ended up going back in, and she stopped the meeting. I rarely speak about my issues, but that day I let everyone know why I'd left. For the next few hours, Bonnie and these six souls prophesied and prayed over me, and then I prophesied and prayed over each of them.

You can't be filled with the Spirit of God and continue as you were before. "Then the Spirit of the LORD will come upon you, and you will prophesy with them and be turned into another man" (1 Samuel 10:6).

Because of my sensory condition, I grew up without any friends. When I came to the Lord and began to grow in my faith, it was the Holy Spirit who was my best friend. I believed that the Holy Spirit could speak, because I'd heard Him many times before. But on this warm July day at Bonnie's house, something special happened. From that day forward, I began to hear the Holy Spirit every day.

To hear the Lord, you must be willing to wait until He speaks to you. Jesus taught us, "My sheep hear My voice, and I know them, and they follow Me" (John 10:27).

After this day, I'd pray each morning that the Holy Spirit would speak to me, and every morning He would. I then posted it online as a devotion. This has never stopped to this day, almost eight years later (as of the time of this writing). I'm always so careful to separate out my own voice, so I sit quietly and wait for His. In all these years, He has never disappointed me.

If the Holy Spirit has come upon you, then the power of God is in you. The Lord Jesus promised, "You will receive power and ability when the Holy Spirit comes upon you" (Acts 1:8 AMP).

I wouldn't be writing devotions, blogs, or books if it weren't for the blessing of hearing the Holy Spirit. The Holy Spirit can bring to you a life you could never imagine. Stop thinking the promises of God aren't for you. Believe that God can speak to you, then wait on Him until He does. Sit quietly in His presence. Listen for His still small voice.

The intentions of God are always good, and His promises are always true. "I will give you a new heart and put a new spirit inside you.... I will put my Spirit inside you" (Ezekiel 36:26-27 CJB).

My prayer is that you would hear the Holy Spirit. My desire is that you'll believe and draw near to the Holy Spirit as your helper and your friend. Whatever has hindered you from fulfilling this great blessing in your life, my hope is that it will be lifted, and that you'll be touched by the Spirit of God. Stop thinking that the filling of the Holy Spirit is a gift for only the few. Know that God's intention and promise is that the Holy Spirit is for us all.

You won't get anything more until you won't settle for anything less. "And when they had prayed, the place where they were assembled together was shaken; and they were all filled with the Holy Spirit" (Acts 4:31).

Perhaps you're like me and are isolated for some reason. This is a great blessing that God has caused you to be all alone with Himself. Perhaps you don't have friends. This is a great blessing, because then the Holy Spirit can be your best friend. Perhaps you have some condition that causes you to suffer. Don't be bitter, but only ask your Father to show you how He's shaping you through your circumstances. God never makes a mistake, and we must trust Him with all that He's doing. This doesn't mean we don't try to make things better, but we trust Him right where we are.

Sometimes when God doesn't explain Himself, He's teaching you to trust Him. "Jesus replied, 'You don't understand now what I am doing, but someday you will'" (John 13:7 NLT).

Over the years, I've never missed hearing from the Holy Spirit each morning and posting a devotion. But our faith journey has hills and valleys and struggles along the way. There are times when I can barely hear Him. There are other days in which the words seem to flow like a river. I've had mornings where I had to press in for an hour until I finally surrendered that I might hear Him. I've come to learn that my striving is a hindrance and my efforts a waste of time. How hard it is to surrender, until we finally do.

There are more Christians willing to serve Christ than surrender to Him. "Then Jesus said to his disciples, 'If any of you wants to be my follower, you must give up your own way, take up your cross, and follow me'" (Matthew 16:24 NLT).

We must be careful when we desire a blessing from the Lord. His favor often comes at a very high price. Consider all that His prophets suffered, then ask if you're ready to do the same.

The more we get the Lord in our life, the more we must give up the right over ourselves. This is a hard decision to make, because it goes against what our flesh wants. This is why Jesus didn't tell us to change ourselves, but to die to ourselves—because there's no negotiating with your former life. Most will not do it, and that's why there's only a remnant who will. Dare to be part of the remnant. Dare to be that one in your circle of influence who goes on to higher levels with God. Dare to be filled with the Spirit of God.

The more you give your life to God, the less you must worry about. "Commit everything you do to the LORD. Trust him, and he will help you" (Psalm 37:5 NLT).

Prayers

* *Heavenly Father, You promised in Your Word that You would fill me with Your Spirit and cause me to live a life of obedience to You. Fulfill that promise in me, I pray.*

* *Lord Jesus, You promised that the Holy Spirit would come and lead me and teach me in the way I should live. Fulfill that promise for me, I pray.*

* *Holy Spirit, thank You for being my friend and for teaching me and speaking to me, guiding me in the way I should go. Help me to hear You more clearly every day.*

Spiritual Growth

* **Know the Holy Spirit:** Learn about the Holy Spirit and all He can do in your faith journey. Jesus sent the Holy Spirit to be our teacher. If you want to learn spiritual things, you need the Holy Spirit as your teacher. Pray for Him to teach you. *There are some things that only the Holy Spirit can teach you.* The Lord Jesus promised us, "The

Helper, the Holy Spirit whom the Father will send in My name, He will teach you all things, and remind you of all that I said to you" (John 14:26 NASB).

- **Hear the Holy Spirit:** Learn to discern the voice of the Holy Spirit in your life. Believe that He can speak to you and believe that He can do so clearly. And be patient—it's in your trust and in your stillness that you'll hear Him. Whether it be a word or a sign, be careful in how you apply it. *Don't pray only for a sign from God, but also for the discernment to know what it means.* "O LORD, listen to my cry; give me the discerning mind you promised" (Psalm 119:169 NLT).

- **Yield to the Holy Spirit:** In your life, as you're given opportunity to minister to others, pray to the Holy Spirit to guide you and show you all that you should do. The more you're willing to yield to the Holy Spirit, the more God will be able to use you. Minister to one person at a time—to whomever the Lord has placed in front of you. *The greater the yielding to the Holy Spirit, the greater the filling of the Holy Spirit.* "If we live by the [Holy] Spirit, let us also walk by the Spirit. [If by the Holy Spirit we have our life in God, let us go forward walking in line, our conduct controlled by the Spirit]" (Galatians 5:25 AMPC). *You must empty a cup that it would be filled with something new.*

14

Keep the Faith

When we pray to God, there's nothing we can ask for that He can't do.

Jesus prayed, "'Abba!' (that is, 'Dear Father!') 'All things are possible for you'" (Mark 14:36 CJB).

IF YOU CAN BELIEVE GOD is faithful, you'll keep the faith regardless of the circumstance you find yourself in.

It's one thing to build up our faith and another to keep the faith in the face of difficulties. Sometimes the things that challenge our faith are not even that big, but they can become like the last straw in a series of disappointments or frustrations. In our faith journey we must do two things: grow in our faith and then keep the faith. It will be as you learn to keep the faith that your faith will grow. Your life will be like a tree in a garden, grounded in faith and producing fruit for the kingdom.

If you want to have a growing faith, you must have a grounded faith. "And now just as you trusted Christ to save you, trust him, too, for each day's problems; live in vital union with him. Let your roots grow down into him and draw up nourishment from him. See that you go on growing in the Lord, and become strong and vigorous in the truth you were taught" (Colossians 2:6-8 TLB).

The Father wants us to be so full of faith that whether or not things go the way we want, our faith remains strong that He's in control over every situation. We can trust His sovereign power in even the smallest of things in our lives. Faith should have no boundary and no limits in believing all that God can do.

Keep the faith in the small things and in the big things, and your life with God will flourish. As you keep the faith, you'll stir up the faith in the life of believers around you.

Jesus brings His power to the table; it's your faith that's needed to pick it up. "And Jesus said to him, 'Go, for your faith has healed you.' Instantly the man could see, and he followed Jesus down the road" (Mark 10:52 NLT).

For fourteen years, I worked in Prison Fellowship Ministries. For the last seven of those years, I was going into several prisons. I'd serve however I was needed, and I was so blessed in all that I was privileged to do. I met so many blessed souls who poured into my life, opening up opportunities and enriching me with their spiritual wisdom.

Every person the Lord places in your path is put there for a reason. Every appointment is a divine appointment when your life is in the hands of God.

Never doubt that a divine Lord arranges divine appointments. Nothing ever happens by chance. Everything has a meaning, and all things have a purpose. "The steps of a [good and righteous] man are directed and established by the Lord, and He delights in his way [and blesses his path]" (Psalm 37:23 AMP).

One time, there was a special event being held at the California Institution for Women state prison that I sometimes served in. There was a guest speaker coming, and her name was Kay Warren. Kay's husband, Rick Warren, had become well known by this time as the senior pastor for Saddleback Church and the author of a bestselling book, *The Purpose Driven Life*. Kay was coming into the prison to give a message of hope to the women there. I wasn't needed for anything at this program, but I was blessed to get invited there anyway. You never know what God is up to, but you can always know that He's up to something.

As soon as you acknowledge God in something, He is. "In all your ways acknowledge Him, and He shall direct your paths" (Proverbs 3:6).

The prison event was on a weekday, so I drove out to the prison after work. It was about twenty-five miles from my work to the prison through the most gridlocked freeway in my area. I was supposed to meet everyone at the prison gate at 6:00 p.m. sharp to get processed in. I left my work at 4:00 p.m. so I'd have two hours to travel that short distance. I'd leave early like this several days each week, going to different prison programs. I was so blessed by all the extra time to study Scripture, as I'd usually get there with much time to spare. When you work for God, you should never get to work late.

How you spend your time reveals what you value most. Jesus taught, "For where your treasure is, there your heart will be also" (Matthew 6:21).

Soon after I got onto the freeway, all the traffic came to a complete stop. This wasn't a normal traffic jam. Every lane and every car just stopped, and nobody was moving. I wondered if perhaps there was an accident. After some time, I was wondering if one or two lanes might start to move, which is often the case after an accident. But nothing was moving. Everybody turned off their car engines, and we were all just waiting. The freeway was blocked coming the other way as well. It was very strange. I found out later that a large van had been parked by the freeway, the windows were covered, and the police thought it might have had a bomb inside.

In the balance sheet of heaven, even when you lose there'll still be a profit. "And we know that all that happens to us is working for our good if we love God and are fitting into his plans" (Romans 8:28 TLB).

I started to pray and thank God for all He was doing, even those things I couldn't see. I was sitting there praying for a long time. All the extra time I'd given myself to get to the prison on time was about used up. I was now at the point where even on a clear day on the freeway, I couldn't make it there on time. Since I wasn't going to make it, I started praying for the women who would be at the event that night. I started to ask the Lord to open their hearts to all the words Kay Warren would say to them.

If you want to stand in the gap, you have to get closer to God. It's the intercessor alone who can plead with God to change the course of history. The Lord said, "So I sought for a man among them who would make a wall, and stand in the gap before Me" (Ezekiel 22:30).

I continued praying on this for quite some time. Prayer is such a privilege. I asked the Lord to put an anointing on Kay as she delivered her message of hope. If you want your own ministry to be blessed, you must pray blessings for the ministries of those around you. Sometimes God's plans put us in situations where prayer is our only option, and there we can tap into the resources of heaven. It's the unseen prayers that move more things for the kingdom than all the workers who are on display.

The more you try to accomplish apart from prayer, the less you'll accomplish. "The earnest prayer of a righteous person has great power and produces wonderful results" (James 5:16 NLT).

Suddenly the cars on the freeway began to move. I had ten minutes to go—ten miles on the worst freeway I know, then a dozen traffic signals along several clogged two-lane roads. I started driving and just prayed a prayer of faith. I prayed that the sea of cars in front of me would part like the Red Sea—and they did, and I was able to go quickly down the freeway. This doesn't happen in my area! I prayed that the Lord would make a way for me to enter into the prison gates even at the exact deadline of 6:00 p.m., though even on a good day I could never have made it. But I've learned that a prayer of faith believes even in the face of the impossible.

The proof of your faith is found in the confidence of your prayers. "Now this is the confidence that we have in Him, that if we ask anything according to His will, He hears us" (1 John 5:14).

I prayed for green lights as I got off the freeway, and every light was green. As I pulled into the prison parking lot, I looked down at the clock, and it was exactly 6:00 p.m. I think God delights in surprising us with answered prayers. I was able to get to the gate and be processed in with everyone else who came for this event. We went to the gym which was set up for this program, and we started getting ready for all the women prisoners to be released from their units for this service. What joy it is to serve the Lord in whatever way He might use us.

The most significant thing you can do is in doing every small thing God calls you to do. "So we keep on praying for you, asking our God to enable you to live a life worthy of his call. May he give you the power to accomplish all the good things your faith prompts you to do" (2 Thessalonians 1:11 NLT).

I found out that the person who was supposed to come with Kay to open up in prayer wasn't able to make it. They asked me if I'd open up the program in prayer. What great privileges the Lord sometimes allows us to have! And what wonderful ways our Father prepares us to serve in His kingdom. All I did that night was repeat some of the prayers that I'd already spoken when I was stuck on the freeway, thinking I wouldn't make it. Learn to see how God is using everything for His purposes.

You can't even dream to the limit of what God can do. "Now to Him who is able to do exceedingly abundantly above all that we ask or think, according to the power that works in us" (Ephesians 3:20).

God had prepared me. God can prepare you too. The Lord doesn't need people with talent but people with faith. We need more faith. We need to believe in a God who can do anything. We need to trust Him no matter how things work out. We need to show the world that our faith is real. All we need is a little faith, and then we can move mountains. The faith we live is the faith we show, and the world is ever watching.

If you want to set a good example as a believer, you must believe.

The test of our faith is not in arguing what we believe but in living it. It's not what you say, but what you live. You live what you believe. Jesus promised, "I tell you this timeless truth: The person who follows me in faith, believing in me, will do the same mighty miracles that I do— even greater miracles than these because I go to be with my Father!" (John 14:12 TPT).

I'll never forget the message Kay gave that night. It was called "Treasures in the Darkness." It was her story of enduring many years with her son's depression. It was a message of hope, a message of keeping the faith even during the darkest times of our lives. We often never know what's going on in the heart of another believer. But on rare occasions the veil will be lifted, and we're most blessed to see the inner heart of a man or a woman, so that it touches our own heart. Be willing to share your own story so you can be a blessing to others.

We think that every good thing is from God and all suffering is of the devil. Yet God uses suffering for our gain, and the devil uses the good pleasures of life for our demise. "I will give you treasures hidden in dark and secret places. Then you will know that I, the Lord God of Israel, have called you by name" (Isaiah 45:3 CEV).

Prayers

* *Heavenly Father, pour into me a faith that will not falter, a faith that will not yield to fear and doubt. Help me stand firm on the foundation of my faith against all odds.*

* *Lord Jesus, help me trust You in every situation, even when I don't understand, knowing that You're with me and You love me and have a purpose and a plan.*

* *Holy Spirit, teach me to trust in the Father's perfect timing. Help me see that He has a plan even when I don't know what that plan might be.*

Spiritual Growth

* **Pray instead of complaining:** Whenever you get the urge to complain about a situation, start to pray for it instead. The circumstances you're in will prepare you for where He's taking you next. How you respond to your circumstances can be a ministry and an encouragement to those around you. *As long as prayer is your last resort, you stand alone on the front lines of your circumstances. The Lord can't go before you if you only keep Him in your back pocket.*

"Don't be afraid, for the LORD will go before you and will be with you; he will not fail nor forsake you" (Deuteronomy 31:8 TLB).

- **Be a prayer warrior:** Be the prayer warrior God wants you to be. Be the intercessor that people around you so desperately need you to be. Believe that God can do anything, then let your prayers begin to flow to that degree—and watch for the miracles that follow. *Miracles don't increase our faith; they reveal our faith. We pray to the degree that we believe.* Jesus promised, "Everything you pray for with the fullness of faith you will receive!" (Matthew 21:22 TPT).

- **Keep the faith:** Determine in your mind that nothing is impossible for the God you serve. Set your mind on God's power and strength, and don't put your eyes only on the problem before you. Look to Jesus, and He'll take care of the storm. Be determined to keep your faith, so that your faith keeps you safe in the hands of God. *The word "impossible" doesn't appear in the dictionaries of heaven.* "Jesus looked at them and said, 'With men it is impossible, but not with God; for with God all things are possible'" (Mark 10:27).

15

Faith over Fear

Faith is to fear what light is to darkness.

"When I am afraid, I will put my trust in you. I praise God for what he has promised. I trust in God, so why should I be afraid? What can mere mortals do to me?" (Psalm 56:3-4 NLT).

IF YOU CAN BELIEVE the Lord is always with you, you won't fear for those things or those people who come up against you.

There are two things that challenge our faith and make it hard to believe that God will help us. The first is fear of the known, when we're faced with a circumstance that overwhelms us. The second is fear of the unknown, when we don't know what will happen, but we fear the worst because that's where our mind takes us.

Only faith can overcome your fear, because only faith puts your confidence in the Lord and all that He can do.

Once you realize that the Lord has you, even fear will be afraid to go near you. "I sought the Lord, and He heard me, and delivered me from all my fears" (Psalm 34:4).

Many of the doubts we entertain were introduced to us by some fear that came upon us. In our fear, we start to doubt that the Lord will help us. We allow doubt to rule over us, and when we do, doubt will always bring more fear. Doubt leads to anxiety, and anxiety leads to more fear, and the fear will only get worse. We start to fear our own shadow, and our minds begin to imagine situations and things that aren't even there.

God doesn't want us to be in bondage to fear, but to be set free in our faith, knowing that He'll never leave us. Fear will diminish only as our faith begins to rise higher.

With God on your side, it's the other side that needs to worry. "If God has determined to stand with us, tell me, who then could ever stand against us?" (Romans 8:31 TPT).

The Lord allows things in our life that can cause us to fear. These fears are to help us grow in our faith. If we have nothing to fear, we have little reason to have faith. Fear can be the catalyst for faith, and that faith will then become your shield from fear. But this doesn't come naturally. We must believe more, so that we fear less—and to do that requires us to trust in what we can't see. We must believe God is with us even though we don't see Him, and often we don't hear Him.

Faith must rule over feelings, not the other way around.

As long as your faith is built upon your feelings, you're standing on shaky ground. "The heart is deceitful above all things, and desperately wicked; who can know it?" (Jeremiah 17:9).

Fear is supposed to help us, as it's what keeps us safe from harm. Fear of getting burned causes us to be safer around fire. But what often happens is that fear is set loose in our minds and we can't keep it contained. Our thoughts feed the fear, and the fear grows ever stronger inside us. The fear that's meant to save us grows to where it begins to hurt us.

Once fear grows larger than your faith, your life becomes overwhelming. The Lord may put us in a circumstance where we're afraid, but He never puts the spirit of fear in us. The Lord wants to draw out our faith so that fear will not rule over us.

Fear is the servant of the devil, but power and love are from the Lord. "For God has not given us a spirit of fear, but of power and of love and of a sound mind" (2 Timothy 1:7).

The Lord had done a great miracle in my life, getting me a new job near the prisons where I ministered. It was working out so well, because I could leave work at my normal time and still get to the prison ministry programs for the evening sessions on time. Yet one thing I've learned over the years is that even in the blessings from God, there are many trials we must go through. This job was no exception. It turned out to be a hostile company where people didn't last very long. We burned through the whole leadership team in under two years, with entire departments changing over in the same period of time. I saw one management role change seven times in under two years. It was hard not to worry at a place like that.

Faith doesn't mean you'll never worry, but that you don't have to. "Don't be afraid, for I am with you; don't be distressed, for I am your God. I give you strength, I give you help, I support you with my victorious right hand" (Isaiah 41:10 CJB).

The general manager over this division was not a nice man. He was unstable in his behavior and threatening in his words. He seemed to enjoy making people feel afraid, and in his arrogance he thought himself the great leader in this behavior. It's in the pride of people where the worst acts of unkindness are born.

We can't change how people treat us, but we can change how we respond to them, and we can change how we treat others. Focus on what you can change, and leave the rest to God.

The more you trust in Him, the less you'll worry about the world. "Listen to me, you people who know righteousness, you people who have my teachings in your hearts. Don't be afraid of being insulted by people. Don't be discouraged by their ridicule" (Isaiah 51:7 NOG).

There was one day when this manager was completely losing it. He was threatening me and another man with losing our jobs. He was demanding that we implement some new software to help prevent damage to aerospace parts being machined at our factory. He didn't need to threaten us to get this done, but I think threatening was the only leadership approach he knew. We have many bullies in the workplace, and they take out their aggression on those around them. After his rant against us, I drove home at the end of the day worried that I might lose my job. Fear crept in, and my faith was being tested.

Don't fear men; fear for men. They've no idea of the God who goes before you. "The LORD your God, who goes before you, He will fight for you" (Deuteronomy 1:30).

Never doubt that the Lord puts you in circumstances to test you. Know that God isn't surprised when people come against you. In the plans of God, He is forming you in the things you're going through.

The next day, while driving to work, I started to consider all that could go wrong. I started praying to the Lord about everything I thought was in front of me. I could lose my job. I could struggle in finding another job. I could lose my income and therefore lose my house. I could even get to where I couldn't buy any food and might starve to death.

Isn't it crazy how our mind can go from faith to fear in one second flat? We can imagine the worst story ahead with only a few words behind it.

Don't focus on those who come against you, but only on the Lord who goes before you. "Therefore understand today that the LORD your God is He who goes over before you as a consuming fire" (Deuteronomy 9:3).

There I was, letting my fears rule me. Right then in my prayer, the Holy Spirit whispered into my heart, *"Even if you die, the worst that can happen is that you'll go to heaven."* This truth has been a faith-changer in my life ever since.

We worry ourselves to death when the Lord has promised us eternal life. God created all things, and He saved you for all eternity, so be sure He can provide for your needs day by day. And even if He doesn't, the worst that can happen is you'll be with Him in heaven.

The Lord has you for all eternity, so why worry about a couple of days or a handful of years? He has you. "The LORD shall preserve your going out and your coming in from this time forth, and even forevermore" (Psalm 121:8).

During the rest of my drive to work, I was speaking out faith-building memories before the Lord. I started to recount all the wonderful victories the Lord had accomplished in my life. How He found this job for me. How He filled me with the ability to teach in prison. How He answered my prayers for healing. How He'd never failed me. I just went on and on, and as I did, my faith began to rise even more.

When we believe for more, we'll fear less, because we're reminded of all that God can do for us.

To build your faith going forward, remember what God has done in the past. "I recall all you have done, O LORD; I remember your wonderful deeds of long ago. They are constantly in my thoughts. I cannot stop thinking about your mighty works" (Psalm 77:11-12 NLT).

It wasn't too long after this that this mean manager was fired. They called me into the office while they were letting him go so that we could transfer some data from his work phone. He wasn't being arrogant with me that day. Perhaps the Lord was doing a work in his heart.

Later I ended up being promoted at this job far beyond what I'd ever expected. But no matter what had happened, God is sovereign, and we can believe that He's with us.

There's not always a happy ending for us on earth, but in heaven we'll all have overwhelming joy when we get there.

The Lord has to test your faith to build your faith, for there's no other way. "Be assured that the testing of your faith [through experience] produces endurance [leading to spiritual maturity, and inner peace]. And let endurance have its perfect result and do a thorough work, so that you may be perfect and completely developed [in your faith], lacking in nothing" (James 1:3-4 AMP).

We all go through difficult times. I pray that in whatever you're going through, and in however fear may be creeping into your life, you'll gain the faith to overcome. Get into the Word of God and pray the promises that He's always with you. Get into prayer and surrender all your life to Him, knowing that you're safe in His hands. Cry out to your Father and know that He hears you. Pray for a faith that's bigger than your fears and believe that He can help you get there.

Sometimes God leaves us in a circumstance until we've learned the lesson. "Remember how the LORD your God led you through the wilderness for these forty years, humbling you and testing you to prove your character, and to find out whether or not you would obey his commands" (Deuteronomy 8:2 NLT).

When we trust in the Lord, we must no longer fear what man might do to us. God is sovereign, and nothing and nobody can touch you unless He allows it. And be sure that even if He allows trouble in your life, He's still with you, and He always has your eternal best interests in mind.

Believe more and fear less, so that your life is an example for the kingdom. Some of your trials are so that others can learn from you how to endure and how to overcome.

Never fear what the Lord has for you. If the Lord is calling you to something, be sure that He'll help you in it. "I am Yahweh, your mighty God! I grip your right hand and won't let you go! I whisper to you: 'Don't be afraid; I am here to help you!'" (Isaiah 41:13 TPT).

Prayers

✶ *Heavenly Father, help me to have a faith that's greater than my fears, so that I look to You and believe that no matter how difficult things may be, You will always help me.*

✶ *Lord Jesus, help me look to You and not to my circumstances, so that when the storms are raging in my life, I can walk on the water as long as I'm looking to You.*

✶ *Holy Spirit, guide me to remember all that You've done for me and all that You can yet do, so that my fears diminish in front me as I remember all You've done before.*

Spiritual Growth

✶ **Seek Him in your fears:** In whatever you fear most right now, seek the Lord and how He would have you grow from it. God doesn't allow trouble in your life unless He means it to change your life. Keep praying for an answer, and trust Him until you get one. *The question is not whether you'll survive the circumstance* *you're in—but whether you'll trust Him through it. The drought reveals the roots.* "Blessed is the man who trusts in the LORD, and whose hope is the LORD. For he shall be like a tree planted by the waters, which spreads out its roots by the river, and will not fear when heat comes; but its leaf will be green, and will not be anxious in the year of drought, nor will cease from yielding fruit" (Jeremiah 17:7-8).

✳ **Make a victory list:** Put together your victory list—those things the Lord has done for you before. Write a list of how He has answered prayers, delivered you from something, or helped someone you loved. Keep this list where you can easily find it later. Then when fear rises within you, pray this list back to God, and watch your faith grow in the process. *In remembering all that God has done, we can trust Him with all that lies ahead.* "I will lift up my eyes to the hills—From whence comes my help? My help comes from the LORD, who made heaven and earth" (Psalm 121:1-2). *You have to be in the valley to look up to the hills.*

✳ **Lose the bitterness:** Don't let the difficulties and hard times in your past make you bitter. Don't become focused only on what's wrong right now so that you miss everything that's right. Rebuke all your thoughts of anger and bitterness, and put your hope in the Lord Jesus. *You'll have as much bitterness in your life as you choose to hold onto.* "Get rid of all bitterness, rage, anger, harsh words, and slander, as well as all types of evil behavior. Instead, be kind to each other, tenderhearted, forgiving one another, just as God through Christ has forgiven you" (Ephesians 4:31-32 NLT).

16

A Faith That Heals

Belief is like a doorway–the wider it's swung open, the greater the flow of the power of God.

"Then Jesus said to him, 'Receive your sight; your faith has made you well'" (Luke 18:42).

IF YOU CAN BELIEVE that Jesus has the power to heal anything, you'll reach out and take hold of this healing for yourself or for those around you.

Over and over we see in Holy Scripture that when the Lord Jesus healed somebody, His power flowed through their faith. It's not that our faith has the power, but only that it opens the way for His power to pour out.

When a woman who had bled for twelve years had the faith to reach out and touch the clothing of Christ, she was healed. "The woman had heard about Jesus, so she came up behind him in the crowd and barely touched his clothes. She had said to herself, 'If I can just touch his clothes, I will get well.' As soon as she touched them, her bleeding stopped, and she knew she was well" (Mark 5:27-29 CEV).

In that crowd there were many who had afflictions. But it was the woman who believed who was willing to step forward and receive her healing. It was the woman who didn't just say she believed, but who reached out and touched even the clothing Jesus wore.

Do you believe enough to grab hold of Christ's clothing today? You'll be willing to grab hold once you believe His power will heal you.

When you're tapping into the resources of heaven, there'll be nothing on earth that can stop you. Jesus blessed the faith of this woman, telling her, "Daughter, your faith has made you well. Go in peace, and be healed of your affliction" (Mark 5:34).

Some years back, I went into a prison to teach a program. I escorted a younger man in with me. He was such a gifted young man, knowledgeable about the Word and able to teach on it so eloquently. He walked and talked with an air of confidence in all that he was doing.

Some people in ministry bring so much of their natural talent with them. I was often jealous, because in my natural self I'm simply not very gifted. Over the years many of those I've ministered with had so much more charm and talent than me. But God doesn't care two cents about your charm or talent; He looks for your surrendered heart. You don't have to worry about what you can't do when you trust in all that He can do. Don't ever let your weaknesses hinder your ministry, because it's there the Lord can use you.

The Lord's power is greater in your weakness. Jesus said, "My grace is sufficient for you, for My strength is made perfect in weakness" (2 Corinthians 12:9).

This young man opened up the program at the chapel. He had a short message already prepared, and he was so impressive with how he presented it. He had many verses memorized and his oratory skills were powerful. He knew how to drive a point home with his body language. His passion was intense. He gave a wonderful message. But he lacked one thing—faith.

You can know Scripture inside out, but apart from faith, it will have no power for you. "The word that they heard did not profit them, not being mixed with faith" (Hebrews 4:2).

After this young man finished, I stepped up to teach the class for the evening. But after a short time, the Lord had other ideas. I felt the leading of the Holy Spirit to go another way, so I put down my notes for the rest of the lesson.

The Holy Spirit can lead you only if you follow. And you'll follow only if you believe that He'll lead you.

The best lessons we can learn in our faith come directly from the Lord we're supposed to believe in. People will proclaim that "God is with us," but then run their programs as if He isn't there.

Stop organizing the Holy Spirit out of your services and out of your life. If you never leave room for Him, don't be surprised when He doesn't show up. "And suddenly there came a sound from heaven, as of a rushing mighty wind, and it filled the whole house where they were sitting... And they were all filled with the Holy Spirit" (Acts 2:2,4).

That night the Lord led me to share some words on healing. The prison yard we were in was called the Old Man's Yard. The older men and those with health issues had been shipped into this yard, since it was closer to outside hospitals. They didn't get much medical care there at the prison, so any prayers for healing were always welcomed.

I asked the men if anyone had any sicknesses or injuries they needed us to pray for. If we believe the Lord can heal us, we must be ready to pray with confidence for that healing.

I don't need to prove that my prayers can bring healing; I need only have faith that His power can heal. "If you have faith when you pray for sick people, they will get well. The Lord will heal them" (James 5:15 CEV).

The first man who asked for prayer had just been shipped in from a prison where many men were becoming sick with a lung condition caused from the environment where they were housed. This man also had a severe back injury, and he was unable to stand up straight.

Sometimes prayer requests will challenge our faith because of how severe the problem is before us. But that's the time to press in and believe more, so that you can receive more of all that God might do. Don't look at the problem, but at the One who can bring the solution.

We can pray for any condition knowing Jesus can bring the cure. "Then Jesus went about all the cities and villages...healing every sickness and every disease among the people" (Matthew 9:35).

The men in the class and I all gathered around this man who was needing prayer. We laid hands on him and started to take turns praying. The prayers being spoken were with authority and confidence of all that the Lord can do. Men were taking turns praying, while others were speaking in their heavenly language.

Never be afraid to speak in the language God puts within you. When God's children can come together in unity and with faith, the windows of heaven are opened, and the blessings will begin to pour down.

You will not get healing by a feeling, but only by believing. "Jesus said to him, 'Go your way; your faith has made you well.' And immediately he received his sight and followed Jesus on the road" (Mark 10:52).

One moment from this night has stood out for me to this day. I looked up and saw at the outer edge of the classroom the young man who'd come into the prison to minister with me. It was the man who had such confidence in himself and in his ability to speak in front of others. In his face I saw fear of what was happening before him. He saw the faith these men had, and it was something I don't think he'd ever seen before.

When the Spirit of God falls on a meeting, the power of man must shrink to the side.

This man knew what to do on his own power, but he was completely unsure what to do when standing before the power of God. This was not to his shame, but to all our shame—as we've all been there. And some of us still remain there.

The problem today with most believers is that they don't believe. We don't need more smarter Christians, we need more believing Christians. "And he [Jesus] was amazed at their unbelief" (Mark 6:6 NLT).

Doubt is our enemy, and faith is our friend. We can say we believe in Jesus, but do we believe what He can do? Overcoming unbelief is the work every Christian must undertake in their faith journey. We all have doubts, and we all need more faith. But getting rid of unbelief doesn't just happen; it must be an ongoing exercise, so that your faith grows. Speak your faith out loud toward God whenever your unbelief tries to overtake you. Believe in God more than your own ability to figure something out. Be determined to believe higher.

The greatest hindrance of God's power in your life is your unbelief. "Now He [Jesus] did not do many mighty works there because of their unbelief" (Matthew 13:58).

We had another inmate there who I'd known for several months, and he asked for prayer. His name was Bob. He was an older man, and he was suffering from pneumonia and having a difficult time trying to breathe. I think that when prayer is our only chance, we pour far more into it. We gathered around this man and started to pray with the power and urgency in all that we were asking for. We were laying hands on him and praying in the power of the Holy Ghost.

When we pray in the Spirit deeply, an anointing pours out from us and onto the person we're laying hands on. Never doubt the power of God and all that He can do through you.

Sometimes God puts a problem before you so He can reveal His power through you. Jesus prophesied, "These signs will accompany those who have believed: in My name...they will lay hands on the sick, and they will recover" (Mark 16:17-18 NASB).

This was such a blessed time of fervent prayer. There was nothing planned and nothing scripted—only the power of God turned loose in the middle of a prayer meeting. We'd be better off with more programs planned by the Lord than by man.

After we finished, and all the inmates went back to their units, I left with this young man who'd come to minister with me. We didn't speak about the experience. Often it's the silence that proves the Holy Spirit is doing a work. How much we all need to be moved to believe with a greater faith. We must all know that no matter how much we believe today, we can believe for more tomorrow.

It takes the most brilliant minds on earth to debate the Word, but it's in the faith like a child to just believe in it. Jesus promised, "Whoever does not receive the kingdom of God as a little child will by no means enter it" (Mark 10:15). *Young children don't question their father. They just believe what he tells them.*

The next week I went to the prison and found out that Bob had been completely healed on that night we prayed for him. When he woke up the next morning, his lungs were completely cleared. He was so ecstatic, and his faith was filled to overflowing.

When God performs a miracle, our faith is bolstered, and our hearts are filled with joy. We don't always get to find out the great blessings of a prayer we've given, but we can always trust that the Lord is able to answer each one.

When you start believing and start receiving, your life will go from one miracle to the next.

If you can explain everything that happens in your life, you're missing out on the supernatural from God. "Even Simon himself believed; and after being baptized, he continued on with Philip, and as he observed signs and great miracles taking place, he was constantly amazed" (Acts 8:13 NASB).

The other man we prayed for—the man with the lung disease and back problem—was not healed. I hear so many theories on why healing doesn't happen. Some even put the blame on the people being prayed for, that they simply didn't believe enough. We need to just trust the Lord with what He does as well as what He doesn't do. It can be the unanswered prayer that builds faith because we have to believe more even when we don't get it. Sometimes God is using a difficult condition for a greater good. We can always pray for healing as long as breath is in a person, but we must trust that the Lord will do the right thing. We also need to be thankful that there's not always a healing, so that we'll someday make our way to heaven.

Praise God that He will not always heal us, so that we'll someday go to heaven. "For this world is not our home; we are looking forward to our everlasting home in heaven" (Hebrews 13:14 TLB).

Prayers

✢ *Heavenly Father, help me in my unbelief. Help me to believe in all that You can do. Help me to be an example of a believer who trusts in You and believes You can do anything.*

✢ *Lord Jesus, I know there's no illness or injury beyond Your ability to heal. Even death cannot contain You, for Your power has no limits.*

✢ *Holy Spirit, pour into me an overflowing faith, a belief in the power born out of heaven, so I can pray for others to be healed of all that afflicts them.*

Spiritual Growth

- **Pray with a passion:** There are so many who need prayer and who need someone willing to pray for them—someone who not only prays believing but also prays with a passion for who they're praying for. Be that passionate prayer warrior for those around you. If you want to get more done, pray more to the One who can do it. *Don't worry as if God can't help you.* "If I were you, I would go to God and present my case to him. He does great things too marvelous to understand. He performs countless miracles" (Job 5:8-9 NLT).

- **Pray believing:** Whenever you have opportunity, pray for those who need healing. Pray expectantly. Pray believing. Have some verses that help you to bolster your faith and the faith of the one you're praying for. Never carry a burden for the healing, as any healing will come only from God. All you must do is believe that He can do it. *What you believe can accomplish more than what you can do.* "Then Jesus said to the Roman officer, 'Go back home. Because you believed, it has happened.' And the young servant was healed that same hour" (Matthew 8:13 NLT).

- **Keep believing:** When God doesn't heal, there's always a reason. We don't always get to know what the reason is this side of heaven, but we can learn to grow and trust in the One who knows. Don't allow unanswered prayers to lessen your faith; let them bolster your faith so you pray even harder. Learn to love God just as much when you don't understand Him as when you do, and your life will be a blessing to others. *It's easy to trust the Lord until you really have to. Having faith doesn't mean things will happen the way we want; it means they could.* "As Scripture says: 'No eye has seen, no ear has heard, and no mind has imagined the things that God has prepared for those who love him'" (1 Corinthians 2:9 NOG).

17

Spirit Led

If you're led by the Holy Spirit, the path you're on will show it.

"With your ears you will hear a word from behind you: 'This is the way; stay on it, whether you go to the right or the left'" (Isaiah 30:21 CJB).

IF YOU CAN BELIEVE the Holy Spirit can lead you, you'll follow Him wherever He would have you go.

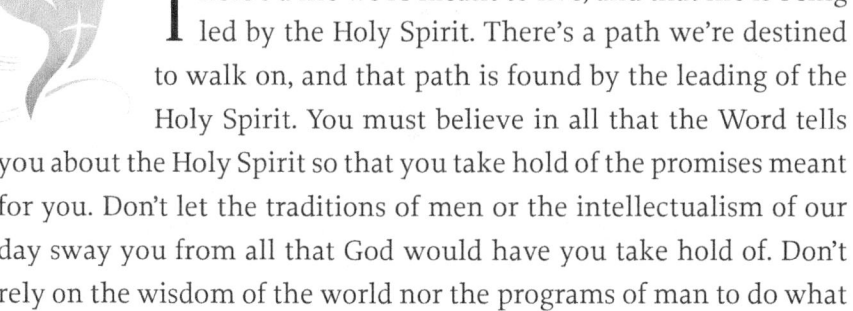

There's a life we're meant to live, and that life is being led by the Holy Spirit. There's a path we're destined to walk on, and that path is found by the leading of the Holy Spirit. You must believe in all that the Word tells you about the Holy Spirit so that you take hold of the promises meant for you. Don't let the traditions of men or the intellectualism of our day sway you from all that God would have you take hold of. Don't rely on the wisdom of the world nor the programs of man to do what only the Holy Spirit can do in your life.

The Holy Spirit will lead us, but it's up to us to follow Him. "For all who are allowing themselves to be led by the Spirit of God are sons of God" (Romans 8:14 AMP).

After many years of serving in the prison ministry, my faith had grown, and the Holy Spirit was leading me like I never imagined possible. My life had fallen into a most wonderful place. I'd been serving in three separate prison facilities for many years, and I was blessed to be getting so many opportunities to teach classes and preach services. I was surrendered to the Lord and relying completely on the Holy Spirit to help me with all I was doing. The Lord was moving in such mighty ways around me that I was simply awestruck. When I went into the prison, it was with expectations of all that the Lord might do.

You cannot be led by the Spirit holding onto the expectations of man. "I did not immediately confer with flesh and blood" (Galatians 1:16).

There was one Saturday afternoon when I was leaving the prison after a full day of ministry, just as I'd been doing for several years. I checked out of the prison and got into my car, and started to drive away. Right then, as I drove past the prison, I got a very clear word from the Lord: *"The prison ministry is going to end for you."* This was in September of 2013, but I can remember His voice like it was yesterday.

You can be inspired by the words of men, but a word from the Lord changes the course of your life. "Be careful to do as the LORD your God has commanded you; you shall not turn aside to the right hand or to the left" (Deuteronomy 5:32).

At this prison, my staff card was renewed every September. For several years, the man who I served with would get the renewal processed through, and I'd go in to get a new picture taken and have a new ID card issued. But with no explanation, I was never given access to go back in again. When the Lord told me it was over, it was over. I didn't understand why, but our understanding isn't required as we serve our Father in heaven. It's our trust that He desires, and our understanding that we must often sacrifice.

Trust the Lord more than your instincts. "Trust in and rely confidently on the LORD with all your heart and do not rely on your own insight or understanding. In all your ways know and acknowledge and recognize Him, and He will make your paths straight and smooth [removing obstacles that block your way]" (Proverbs 3:5-6 AMP).

When I'd ministered in the prison that day, I didn't know it would be my last day there. But I heard the word from the Lord after the program as clearly as if you were speaking right in front of me. We must not question where the Lord leads us, and we must not be disobedient in where He's telling us to go. I believe God is leading His children in countless ways, and if they would only yield to Him, their lives would be forever blessed. We must learn that He seeks our willingness to follow Him in everything.

You can only be guided if you're willing to follow. "If you want to be my disciple, follow me and you will go where I am going. And if you truly follow me as my disciple, the Father will shower his favor upon your life" (John 12:26 TPT).

When I got home that afternoon, I checked the mailbox at my house. There was a letter from the women's prison that I served in, and it was written by the warden's assistant. The letter said that my access to that prison had been revoked, and I could no longer go in there. I found out later that a woman inmate had become pregnant, and so they did a blanket denial of all the males who were coming in doing ministry. How quickly my ministry was coming to an end.

Don't let your expectations get in the way of God's plan for your life. "A man's heart plans his way, but the LORD directs his steps" (Proverbs 16:9).

A few weeks later, I got a letter from the last prison I was serving in. They were introducing new rules that would likely disqualify me from coming in. The word I'd received from the Lord was unfolding very quickly. I could hardly believe what was happening to this ministry that I adored so much. In a single day, the ministry for me ended in two of three prisons I served at. And now it seemed the last prison would not let me renew again.

Sometimes God's plans don't make sense until you see them in the rearview mirror.

Spiritual leading often makes no sense to natural thinking. As God has said, "I will lead them in paths they have not known. I will make darkness light before them, and crooked places straight" (Isaiah 42:16).

I asked the Lord about what He was doing. I wondered why He went to so much trouble to get me to serve inside prisons only to end it. I thought I was doing so much for Him there, so I didn't understand why He would end it. But I trusted in Him all the same, and I kept serving in the last prison. My staff card at that prison would expire in February, so I assumed the ministry would end for me then. I didn't know what would come next after this ministry, but I believed that God would show me. With our calling from the Lord, we only need to know one step at a time.

The greatest thing you can do for God is whatever He calls you to do. "If you do what the LORD wants, he will make certain each step you take is sure. The LORD will hold your hand, and if you stumble, you still won't fall" (Psalm 37:23-24 CEV).

Do you believe the Lord can lead you? Do you believe He has a plan and a purpose for your life? We must first believe before we can walk in His leading, because we'll follow Him only if we believe He's leading us. He won't show you the whole path, because why would you need faith for that? No, He shows you one step at a time, and your faith will cause you to believe that He'll show you the next step when it's time. Don't expect God to show you all that you're not yet ready to receive.

You must believe that the Lord will give you a word before He'll give you a sentence. A large tree is always established with many small roots. Start believing small first, and then your faith can grow. "Abraham never doubted. He believed God, for his faith and trust grew ever stronger, and he praised God for this blessing even before it happened. He was completely sure that God was well able to do anything he promised" (Romans 4:20-21 TLB).

That next February, in 2014, I thought I'd get denied access at the last prison I was still serving in. Instead, my staff card was renewed for another year. I couldn't believe it. It made no sense to me whatsoever. Earlier I'd had a strong word from the Lord that prison ministry would end for me, and it did end for the other two prisons. But this prison signed me up for another year. I kept serving faithfully and was so blessed by all the many things that the Lord was still having me do. Yet I knew what He'd told me about the ministry ending. I prayed to God often, asking Him to reveal to me what He was doing. I wasn't getting any answers for several months. We need to learn to pray with diligence and wait patiently for His answer.

When the world comes against you, this is often when the kingdom is trying to work through you. Press in. If you're in His will, He's on your side. "Don't be lazy when hard work is needed, but serve the Lord with spiritual fervor. Rejoice in your hope, be patient in your troubles, and continue steadfastly in prayer" (Romans 12:11-12 CJB).

One day I was praying to the Lord and asking once again why He told me the ministry was ending when it clearly had not. Finally, after months of silence, I heard a single word from Him: *"Abraham."* I pondered what He meant by that, and the word that jumped into my thoughts was "timing." When the Father spoke a prophetic word to Abraham that he and Sarah would have a child, He never said when. Abraham and Sarah waited many years, and even tried to help the process along by using Hagar as a surrogate. But God had made the promise, and it would come to pass on His timing.

Abraham had to wait twenty-five years for the promise. Why are we in such a hurry? Why do we think prophecy must come in a day?

Prophetic words aren't bound by the timelines of man. "For the vision is yet for an appointed time; but at the end it will speak, and it will not lie. Though it tarries, wait for it; because it will surely come, it will not tarry" (Habakkuk 2:3).

For many more months I never heard another word from the Lord on this topic. I rested in the prison ministry that He still had me serving in, but I wondered how long I would remain there.

We're such impatient creatures, always trying to know the whole plan. But the Lord doesn't work by our rules—we work by His. We must learn that it's not God who should adapt to us, but we who must adapt to Him.

Don't try to get back to where you were, but to where the Lord is taking you. "Stop imitating the ideals and opinions of the culture around you, but be inwardly transformed by the Holy Spirit through a total reformation of how you think. This will empower you to discern God's will as you live a beautiful life, satisfying and perfect in his eyes " (Romans 12:2 TPT).

Faith is built up only where faith is needed. When once your faith is built up high enough, not knowing the whole plan will no longer be a burden. When you believe God has you, you can let go.

The Lord must break you to build you, and He must stretch you to bring an increase. Learn to let the Lord lead you as He chooses, and don't worry along the way. When once you believe He can lead you, then He will—because it's there that you'll follow Him.

If you don't believe God can speak to you, you won't listen for Him. What you believe impacts what you'll do. What you believe impacts what the Lord will do. Believe more, and you'll receive more.

The more you believe, the more you receive, and this will cause you to believe even more. Jesus taught, "I tell you, you can pray for anything, and if you believe that you've received it, it will be yours" (Mark 11:24).

Prayers

✦ *Heavenly Father, thank You for sending Your Son to save me, and for sending Your Holy Spirit to lead me, so I can walk in the path You have for me.*

✦ *Lord Jesus, help me live the surrendered life, so that I'm willing to follow You wherever You take me. Help me trust in Your plans.*

✦ *Holy Spirit, help me focus on the next step You would have me take. Help me to not be concerned about the steps that will follow, but only for the next one, trusting You with all the rest.*

Spiritual Growth

✦ **Trust Him for the next step:** Be satisfied in not knowing all of God's plans for your life. Be willing to take each step as the Holy Spirit leads you. When once you believe God has you, then all you need to serve Him is knowing the next step you should take. Don't get stuck at the starting line while waiting to know how the race will end. *The journey may be long, but it's the decision to go that prevents you from starting.* "Before you do anything, put your trust totally in God and not in yourself. Then every plan you make will succeed" (Proverbs 16:3 TPT).

- **Trust Him enough to wait:** Believe that the Holy Spirit can lead you, and be willing to wait on Him until He does. So often we rush ahead of the Lord and fail to gain His leading, and then the trouble begins. Be willing to lose something on earth that you might gain something from heaven. *The Lord will not show up if you don't wait for Him.* "I waited and waited and waited some more, patiently, knowing God would come through for me. Then, at last, he bent down and listened to my cry" (Psalm 40:1 TPT).

- **Trust His timing:** When the Lord gives you a prophetic word or leading, never add to it the timing of your own design. God's timetables aren't bound by the due dates given by man. Be patient as you're waiting—it's in the waiting that the Lord will prepare you. Often you must wait for as long it takes before you'll yield to Him. *How long will the Lord have to keep you in the belly of a fish until you'll yield yourself to Him?* "Now the Lord had prepared a great fish to swallow Jonah. And Jonah was in the belly of the fish three days and three nights" (Jonah 1:17).

18

The Lion and the Donkey

Don't compromise an inch, and God will give you a mile.

"And the Lord will make you the head and not the tail, and you will only be above, and not be underneath, if you listen to the commandments of the Lord your God which I am commanding you today, to follow them carefully" (Deuteronomy 28:13 NASB).

IF YOU CAN BELIEVE that the Lord has a divine calling on your life, you'll be obedient to His call even when it doesn't make sense.

Before we can follow Him, we must believe that the Lord can lead us. Before we listen for His voice, we must believe that the Holy Spirit will speak to us. And once He speaks and we listen, we must be willing to be obedient to what He's telling us to do. This obedience is not just a matter of doing good, but of doing the thing the Lord is calling you to do. The proof of your faith is when it moves you.

Obedience will open doors for you, but disobedience will slam them shut. "What is more pleasing to the LORD: your burnt offerings and sacrifices or your obedience to his voice? Listen! Obedience is better than sacrifice, and submission is better than offering the fat of rams" (1 Samuel 15:22 NLT).

Often the Lord will give us a clear leading without a clear understanding. This is purposeful in that it then requires your faith for you to take action. Our faith is formed when we must do something without knowing what will happen. We must simply do it, because we trust the One who's telling us what to do.

The more you can act in faith apart from knowing the outcome, the more useful you'll be in the hands of God.

It's not what you know that Jesus is most interested in, but what you believe. Jesus said, "When the Son of Man comes, will He really find faith on the earth?" (Luke 18:8).

The Lord had given me a word in September of 2013, telling me that my prison ministry was going to end. As I explained earlier, right away I was turned away from two of the three prisons I served in. But the third prison renewed me for another year the following February. I wasn't sure why the ministry didn't end as He told me it would. Much later the Lord gave me the word "Abraham," and I sensed that this meant the Lord's word was true, but the time had not yet come. Abraham was given the promise of a son through Sarah, and it was twenty-five years before that promise came true. We must learn to wait on the Lord and to trust in His timing. He makes you wait to test your faith and to help you believe for even more.

Resting in the Lord is the hardest thing we'll ever do, yet it takes the least effort. Resting is trusting in action. Faith isn't revealed in what you can carry but in what you give to the Lord. "Be still and rest in the Lord; wait for Him and patiently lean yourself upon Him" (Psalm 37:7 AMPC).

The following September—a full year after the Lord had first given me the word that the ministry would end—I went home after a long day at work followed by a late-night serving in the prison. I made it home after ten o'clock and rested for a while at my desk, then went to bed. I didn't sleep very long, and soon found myself wide awake at around midnight. I knew the Lord had something for me, and He wasn't going to let me sleep until I received it. This wasn't my first time being wakened in the middle of the night by the Lord.

It's in your exhaustion that the Lord can speak to you, and you don't have the strength to argue back. "When I remember You on my bed, I meditate on You in the night watches, for You have been my help, and in the shadow of Your wings I sing for joy. My soul clings to You; Your right hand takes hold of me" (Psalm 63:6-8 NASB).

I got up and sat at my desk. I started to pray, and after a time, I heard this word from the Lord: *"the lion and the donkey."* It didn't make any sense to me, so I searched for the words *lion* and *donkey* in the Bible. Right off I found the story in 1 Kings 13. I read this story of how God had called a prophet to go do a work. The Lord had instructed this prophet what to do after doing the work—to return home a different way, and to not stop to eat or to drink along the way. Don't question the Lord's commands, and know there's always a reason behind them.

Whenever you get ahead of yourself, you're not following the Lord. "You must follow the Lord your God alone! Revere him! Follow his commandments! Obey his voice! Worship him! Cling to him—no other!" (Deuteronomy 13:4 CEV).

This prophet did as God had told him to do. He found the king and gave him a warning. In his anger, the king pointed to the prophet to have him arrested, and instantly the king's arm withered to nothing. This prophet then healed the king's arm by the power of God.

We should never look at an illness or injury and think it's beyond the healing power of God. The king invited him back to his house to eat, but the prophet said no, because of the command of the Lord to not eat or drink before returning home.

In whatever way God isn't first in your life, you're grossly out of order. Jesus taught us, "You shall love the Lord your God with all your heart, with all your soul, with all your mind, and with all your strength" (Mark 12:30).

Then the prophet started his trek home. On the way, a bad prophet heard of the events and invited the good prophet into his home. He offered food to the man, but the good prophet said no, because of the command of God. But the bad prophet lied and said that God had said it was okay for him to eat. So the man ate. Right then, the bad prophet got a true word from God, and he gave it to the good prophet—that God was going to kill the good prophet because of his disobedience.

The greater your role for God, the greater His judgment will be on your disobedience.

You can't do whatever you want and expect God to bless it. "Blessed is everyone who...walks in His ways" (Psalm 128:1).

The good prophet left to go on his way with his donkey. Along the way, a lion attacked and killed him, leaving him dead on the road. Then the lion sat down next to him on one side, and the donkey sat on the other side. This was a sign from the Lord that this was a supernatural judgment, because a lion would normally eat the prey, and a donkey would normally flee from the presence of a lion.

Then I heard this from the Lord: *"I told you that the prison ministry was going to end, but it will end not by the power of man, but by My command. Man is not kicking you out—I am calling you out."* Right then, I knew that this is why the ministry had continued—that it would not end by the power of man but only by my obedience to the command of God.

Obedience is not by strength but by submission. "Therefore submit to God" (James 4:7).

I then had this powerful feeling of the fear of the Lord. I knew that I had to leave the ministry in obedience to God or face His judgment. In the middle of the night, right then and there at my desk, I wrote my resignation email to the ministry I'd been part of for fourteen years. I gave several months' notice, so they had time to replace me. I sent the email, then went to bed. We can always sleep more soundly when we're obedient to God.

The ending of one season always marks the beginning of another. Live in the hope of tomorrow, not in the losses of yesterday. "There is a season (a time appointed) for everything and a time for every delight and event or purpose under heaven" (Ecclesiastes 3:1 AMP). *The plant lives by the sunlight each day.*

Soon after giving notice, I had someone in the ministry give me a word. They told me that the Lord had told them I was supposed to remain in the prison ministry. A week later, they told me the same thing. It sparked a desire for me to want to stay in the ministry that I loved. It caused a moment of doubt. It was a temptation. But it also shocked me, as I knew the word I'd received, and I was afraid to be disobedient to the Lord.

Fearing the Lord recognizes His absolute power. Loving the Lord recognizes His endless mercies. You can't appreciate one without the other. The essence of the Law is built upon this foundation of fear and love. "And now, Israel, what does the LORD your God require of you, but to fear the LORD your God, to walk in all His ways and to love Him, to serve the LORD your God with all your heart and with all your soul" (Deuteronomy 10:12).

Then I remembered the story of the lion and the donkey, and the bad prophet who lied to serve his own interest. The good prophet listened to the bad prophet over the word of God. This was why the Lord had led me to that story. I just kept quiet with this person who was giving me this word. Know that many in ministry operate believing that the means justify the ends. But in the kingdom, it's all about the means. What we do matters more than the outcomes we're seeking. If the means are wrong, the ends are always tainted.

Later this person told me they knew I'd heard from the Lord because of my resolve. I never said anything. It was not my resolve—it was my fear. People try to redefine fear in the Bible, but fear means fear. Fear the Lord.

Never fear that men might judge you wrongly but that God will judge you rightly. "So then each of us shall give account of himself to God" (Romans 14:12).

In February of 2015, I preached my last service in prison. As had happened many times before, the Lord revealed to me before the service which man would be saved at the altar call. This had happened so many times before I couldn't count them. Each time it was such an amazing experience to know who the Lord would reach on that day. This particular service was so special, since every man there came up to recommit his life to Jesus, and the one man the Lord showed me also came up and received the Lord Jesus Christ into his life. The Lord blessed me with an amazing end to an amazing season of ministry.

I've never been back to a prison since. It broke my heart to leave that ministry, as it was an honor to serve the men and women behind bars. Still, it blessed me to be obedient to God.

Never underestimate the great value of your obedience. Know that His plans are better than yours. Our job is to follow Him, and then He'll lead us in the way we should go.

If you want favor with men, you must walk in obedience to God. The Lord will give you favor with men when it serves His purposes, not yours. "The LORD was with Joseph and showed him mercy, and He gave him favor in the sight of the keeper of the prison" (Genesis 39:21).

I did wonder why the Lord would pull me out of prison ministry when I was serving faithfully and seeing so much fruit come from it. Friend, He had other plans for me. Over time, I saw that it allowed me to write for the kingdom in a way I'd never imagined.

God has a plan for you. Perhaps you're in one of His plans right now. Maybe He's about ready to upset the thing you're in and take you somewhere else. Don't worry about where He might ask you to go, but only be determined in your heart that you'll go wherever He sends you.

God has a calling on your life, but it's up to you to answer Him. Don't seek the title but live the title—so that it would seek you. "And David made himself a name when he returned from killing eighteen thousand Syrians in the Valley of Salt" (2 Samuel 8:13). *God chose David to be a king, but it was up to David to act like one. It's not enough to know your calling; you must also walk in it.*

When you remove the conditions of your service to the Lord, He can expand how much He'll use you. Don't use worldly measurements to determine the degree of effectiveness of your service for the kingdom. God turns the natural on its head when He turns loose His purposes for the kingdom through us. Just believe your Father can use you, and let Him use you however He will—then your life will be a blessing to the kingdom. Don't let your shortcomings prevent you from being filled with His abilities to use you. He made you special, so just be who you are.

God didn't make you like anybody else, so just be yourself. "For You formed my inward parts; You covered me in my mother's womb. I will praise You, for I am fearfully and wonderfully made; marvelous are Your works, and that my soul knows very well" (Psalm 139:13-14).

Prayers

✴ *Heavenly Father, help me hear your directions ever so clearly, and give me the faith and courage to faithfully follow all that You would have me do.*

✴ *Lord Jesus, teach me to trust You with my life, taking every step in my journey knowing that You're with me and for me in everything You would have me do.*

✴ *Holy Spirit, guide me in my calling, so that I go where You would have me go. Help me remove all the conditions, until I'm fully given over to You for the kingdom.*

Spiritual Growth

✴ **Trust Him:** In whatever trial you're in right now, choose this day to trust Him with it. Tell the Lord that you realize He's building your faith as you learn to trust Him in the thing you don't yet understand. *Faith is not a path out of circumstances, but a way through them.* "My brethren, take the prophets, who spoke in the name of the Lord, as an example of suffering and patience" (James 5:10).

✴ **Seek His will:** We serve a sovereign God who has power over everything around us. We serve an all-knowing God who's aware of everything we need to walk in the purposes He has for us. Nothing happens by chance, so look for His hand and His voice in everything going on around you. Be determined that you'll seek His will over your own. *You won't seek God's will while holding onto your own.* "Don't be like the people of this world, but let God change the way you think. Then you will know how to do everything that is good and pleasing to him" (Romans 12:2 CEV).

- **Don't look back:** Press ahead in your faith journey, never trying to go back to where you were before. Remember the good seasons, but keep your eyes fixed on the season you're in now. In whatever the Lord puts in front of you, step into it and trust in His timing. *The Lord wants more for you than you're yet taking hold of.* "Not that I have already obtained it [this goal of being Christlike] or have already been made perfect, but I actively press on so that I may take hold of that [perfection] for which Christ Jesus took hold of me and made me His own" (Philippians 3:12 AMP).

19

Faith Waits

The more you believe in something, the longer you're willing to wait for it.

"Wait for and confidently expect the Lord"
(Psalm 27:14 AMP).

IF YOU CAN BELIEVE that the Lord will come through for you, you'll faithfully wait for Him as long as it takes.

The further you go on with God, the more He'll test your faith. He doesn't test you that you might be found lacking, but so that He can build you up even more. As you believe more, you'll trust more in the ever present help of the Lord. To build up this trust, He'll make you wait. The waiting is the testing of your faith. The longer the wait, the greater the test, and the more help it will be in growing your faith.

The great work of a saint is learning how to rest in God. "Rest in the Lord" (Psalm 37:7). *Your words may say that you trust Jesus, but waiting on Him proves it.*

We need to learn that there are no compartments in our life in which the Lord doesn't belong. Whether it be in our ministry or our secular work, in our marriages or our friendships, the Lord is there to lead us. It's in the most important things in your life that the Lord will test you the most. We worry the most about those things we most fear to lose. God knows what you need, and He knows how He'll provide it. The only question is: Will you trust Him?

Every worry is an opportunity to believe. Faith is not a switch but a dial. "Lord, I believe; help my unbelief!" (Mark 9:24).

I've learned to wait on the Lord, knowing that He'll always lead me if I'm willing to wait for Him to do so. It can be hard to wait because I still see in the natural, and I can see all the obstacles that stand before me. So often I'll be in a situation and want to jump by my instincts more than by the leading of the Lord. Yet I long to be led by the Lord on major decisions in my life so that I'll remain in His will.

The wait can be weeks, months, and even years—but the wait is always worth it. I've been so blessed in the waiting, because it's there that He has proven Himself ever faithful, and my faith has grown the most.

To be led by God you must wait for God. "Lead me in your truth and teach me, for you are the God of my salvation; for you I wait all the day long" (Psalm 25:5 ESV).

I was still working at a job the Lord provided for me so that I could continue to minister in the prisons. But prison ministry had ended for me. And as I was soon to find out, my new job would end also. I was doing well at this job and had just been promoted to a higher position. The day before my promotion was announced, I got a phone call with an offer for a new job somewhere else. I listened to the offer, and it sounded very good. But it made no sense to leave my existing job when I got promoted.

A principle in God's kingdom is that what makes sense on earth isn't always the plan we get from heaven.

When God gives you a calling that makes no sense to the world, you're walking on kingdom principles. "For the Kingdom of God is not just a lot of talk; it is living by God's power" (1 Corinthians 4:20 NLT).

I didn't have much time to decide, so I was praying much about it. Unless I heard a specific word from the Lord, I was determined not to take the new job. I want to live my life trusting God and believing that He can lead me. If He truly was opening a new door, then I believed He could show me the need to step through it.

The problem most of us have is that we see open or closed doors using our natural vision. We need to discern open and closed doors through the promptings of the Holy Spirit.

It takes discernment to know the difference between a distraction and a divine appointment. "Set your gaze on the path before you. With fixed purpose, looking straight ahead, ignore life's distractions. Watch where you're going! Stick to the path of truth, and the road will be safe and smooth before you" (Proverbs 4:25-26 TPT).

A day later, I was at home and I went to lie down for a nap in the afternoon. I was very tired this day, so I fell asleep. The Lord came to me in a dream and told me that if I stayed at my current job, I'd get fired. It isn't typical for me to have the Lord meet me in my dreams, but when He does, it's always with a clear word, and I've always been blessed in my obedience to His leading. I woke up and called about the new job right away to begin the interviewing process. I ended up getting this new job.

Believe that the Lord can lead you and trust in how He would do so.

Never doubt that the Lord will lead you, and be sure that you follow. "Commit everything you do to the Lord. Trust him to help you do it, and he will" (Psalm 37:5 TLB).

This new job was in Boston, and I found myself commuting almost every week from Los Angeles to Boston to work there. About a year later, on one of the flights, I met a young lady named Aejoo Park—she goes by AJ. She and I became friends, and she introduced me to a ministry and many wonderful believers just outside Boston in Cambridge. For the next few years, I was so blessed by the many believers I spent time with there.

Going into the third year at this new job, I saw that it wasn't going to last, yet the Lord wasn't telling me to leave. As we must believe that the Lord will tell us *where* to go, we must also believe that He'll tell us *when*. I just kept praying about it and working hard at my job. I'm convinced that many make the wrong decisions in life because they rely on their own limited perspective instead of waiting on the Lord to lead them. We cannot change the wrong decisions we've made in the past, but we can decide not to do the same thing again in the future.

Never doubt what God can do, and trust Him with His timing. "And we know [with great confidence] that God [who is deeply concerned about us] causes all things to work together [as a plan] for good for those who love God, to those who are called according to His plan and purpose" (Romans 8:28 AMP).

I remember one night in Cambridge spending time with my friend Brian Allwood. He's a doctor from South Africa, and was in Boston for a year on an exchange program. I'd met him and his wife Taytum in Cambridge by a divine appointment several months earlier. We often met when I was traveling there. One night, Brian gave me a prophetic word for why the Lord still had me at this job. He told me, "You're there for the king." This was a good word, as I was there supporting my boss, who'd brought me to Boston. For the next several months, I held onto this prophetic word.

The Lord always has a purpose—but will we see it?

Don't despise the season you're in; just ask God what He would have you do in it. "To everything there is a season, a time for every purpose under heaven...a time to break down, and a time to build up" (Ecclesiastes 3:1,3).

There came a time when my boss turned against me in regard to a certain decision. He was an unbeliever, and was trying to save himself in an impossible situation he was in. Soon after this he was fired. I believe the Lord lifted His protection off my boss after he turned against me.

Know that the Lord is always with you and protecting you in ways you don't even know. We must realize that the Lord can protect us in a situation or allow us to go through things. Learn to trust the Lord in the good times and in the bad.

Don't worry about what lies ahead; just keep your mind focused on the Lord who is with you. "You will keep him in perfect peace, whose mind is stayed on You, because he trusts in You" (Isaiah 26:3).

The company brought in a new boss, and I could tell it wasn't going to go well for me. All the signs pointed the wrong way. But still, the Lord wasn't giving me a word to leave. This went on for a few months. Everything I could see said to leave, but the Lord was silent.

If you want a higher faith, be ready to get the silent treatment. You can't learn to trust more without a reason to trust more. Don't let your circumstances lead you more than the Lord. It's in the face of uncertainty that God will test the certainty of your faith.

Never despair with where you are, but only trust in where He's taking you. "Forget what happened in the past, and do not dwell on events from long ago. I am going to do something new. It is already happening. Don't you recognize it?" (Isaiah 43:18-19 NOG).

A few months later, I was in Cambridge to meet with Brian and Taytum at their apartment. They'd also invited my friend AJ to come over. We had a wonderful dinner and a long evening of fellowship and prayer. I'm always so blessed when I'm around such strong believers. We ended the night praying for one another. I'll never forget AJ prayed a prophetic word over me, that the Lord would bring me revelation on what to do with my job with perfect clarity.

We need to pray more for each other, and all that God can do to help us.

The longer we pray for something, the more it reveals our faith in God. "Be persistent and devoted to prayer, being alert and focused in your prayer life with an attitude of thanksgiving" (Colossians 4:2 AMP).

The next day I went in to meet with my second new boss. The first one had quietly demoted me without even a phone call or a meeting. This second boss seemed to be a nice man. We sat down in his office, then he started to go down the list of things I was responsible for. For each one, he told me who he was shifting that particular responsibility to. When he got to the end of the list, there was nothing left for me. I told him it sounded like there was no job left, and I'd be happy to help with the transition. He just smiled. Sometimes it's the nicest dressed people who are hiding the ugliest hearts. But don't worry about the wicked, because the Lord will deal with them when He's ready.

Don't worry when the wicked are winning, because they're not even in the right race. "Yet a little while and the wicked shall be no more... The Lord laughs at him, for He sees that his day is coming" (Psalm 37:10,13).

I was so happy to finally know it was time for me to go! Isn't God so grand that He answers our prayers so that we know exactly what we need to do? Never fear the leading of the Lord but only the impatience of your heart.

I started to look for a new job that very day. The prayer from AJ that I'd have perfect clarity could not have been answered more perfectly. The more we wait for a thing, the greater we can appreciate it when it comes. Though I had some fear for what was ahead, my faith helped me overcome it.

We're all growing in our faith. Let us share with each other in our struggles. Learn to be open in all you're going through, and it will be a blessing to those around you.

Being genuine is the best version of yourself. "Don't think you are better than you really are. Be honest in your evaluation of yourselves" (Romans 12:3 NLT).

My prayer is that you'll learn to wait on the Lord, and that you discover the blessings of all the Lord would give you in your waiting. I pray that your faith would grow, and that your intimacy with Christ would increase, and that your heart would be full.

Pray believing, and dare to wait on the Lord. I've known many people who don't wait on the Lord, and who come to regret it with all that they suffer. I've known some who wait on the Lord in the face of things that would make anyone want to jump, and they're blessed in their waiting.

If you want to grow in your faith, you must grow in your willingness to wait.

Waiting is trusting in action. "Our soul waits for the LORD; He is our help and our shield" (Psalm 33:20).

When we wait on the Lord Jesus, we enter into a trusting and intimate relationship with Him. As we trust Him more, He'll entrust more to us. He longs to lead us by His Holy Spirit. We must lean into this leading and wait for His directions. Be sure that the waiting is the process by which your faith will grow. The greater the wait you're in, the greater the faith that will follow. Don't worry about your past failures, but only learn from them. Be determined in your mind that you'll follow the Lord from this day forward.

Let waiting be your sacrifice to the Lord. "I waited patiently and expectantly for the LORD; and He inclined to me and heard my cry" (Psalm 40:1 AMPC).

Prayers

✴ *Heavenly Father, give me the wisdom to know those things I need to wait on Your direction for, and grant me patience to faithfully trust You in the waiting.*

✴ *Lord Jesus, You modeled for us a life of submission to the Father, going only when and where He told You to go. By Your power in me, help me to wait for the Father.*

✴ *Holy Spirit, give me the patience and determination in my spirit to wait even when it makes no sense, as I trust You to help me in the waiting.*

Spiritual Growth

✴ **Follow natural lines:** While you're waiting for the leading of the Lord, follow the natural lines along the way. Until you get a new leading, stay in your lane and do the best you can. *Where you lack divine leading, follow natural lines and know that He will help you.* "Trust in the LORD completely, and do not rely on your own opinions. With all your heart rely on him to guide you, and he will lead you in every decision you make. Become intimate with him in whatever you do, and he will lead you wherever you go" (Proverbs 3:5-6 TPT).

✴ **Wait patiently:** Be patient as you wait for things, knowing the Lord will give them to you only when you're ready. You'll grow more and learn more in the waiting, and that's exactly why the Lord will leave you there. Often the waiting period is the length of time it takes us to finally learn what He's trying to teach us. *Patience is more important than effort when doing kingdom work.* "God's servants must not be troublemakers. They must be kind to everyone, and they must be good teachers and very patient" (2 Timothy 2:24 CEV).

* **Journal your journey:** Journal your faith, and record how you're progressing or slipping in your journey. At the end of the day, make a note of where you were submitting to the Lord and where you were striving in your flesh. If you can't see the problem, it will likely never get resolved. *To rest in the Lord requires submission and not effort. It's always in the efforts of man that obstacles to faith arise.* "As for me, I look to the Lord for help. I wait confidently for God to save me, and my God will certainly hear me" (Micah 7:7 NLT).

20

Breath of the Spirit

You need the Holy Spirit in you for the purposes of God to flow from you.

"And when He [Jesus] had said this, He breathed on them, and said to them, 'Receive the Holy Spirit'" (John 20:22).

IF YOU CAN BELIEVE the Lord gives you everything you need for ministry, you'll be confident of always having everything you need to serve Him in your calling.

As I grew in my faith, I wanted even more. The secret to gaining more in the kingdom is to give up more of the world. I had a deep desire to grow more spiritually, and I found the blessed value in fasting. I'd been fasting for many years. I started a pattern that whenever I'd go into the prisons to do ministry, I would fast before going in. Since I was going in several times each week, I was fasting often. One of the most powerful voices of our flesh comes from our stomachs. When we start to make our stomach submissive to our spirit, we begin to strengthen our spiritual man, which then brings more power to our spiritual life.

You need never plead for the Holy Spirit to fill you, but only ask—"that He would grant you, according to the riches of His glory, to be strengthened with might through His Spirit in the inner man...that you may be filled with all the fullness of God" (Ephesians 3:16,19).

During these years after prison ministry, I entered into a more intense pattern of fasting 120 days each year. I'd fast from all food and drink except coffee and water for a twenty-four-hour period, from around sunset to sunset. I'd do this staggered two or three days a week, ten days a month. I don't mention this to promote myself, but to promote this practice which in our day is so often overlooked. If you look back at the anointed men and women of our faith, you'll find there was a life of fasting and consecration to the Lord.

Fasting consecrates you from the world. Praying consecrates you to God. Either by itself is beneficial, but praying and fasting together will change who you are. "So I turned to the Lord God and pleaded with him in prayer and fasting" (Daniel 9:3 NLT).

If you've never entered into a pattern of fasting, I'd encourage you to consider doing so. If you want to gain in the spiritual, you must increase in your control over your natural. Let your faith cost you something. If you want to grow in your faith, you must exercise your faith. There's no exercise more powerful than trusting in God to help you overcome the desires of your flesh. If you think you can't overcome your flesh on your own power, you're right. You need His power, so pray for that.

If you want to walk a higher faith, you have to let go of the lower things. Stop looking at fasting as giving up something good, but rather as gaining something so much greater. The Lord Jesus taught, "When you fast, anoint your head and wash your face, so that you do not appear to men to be fasting, but to your Father who is in the secret place; and your Father who sees in secret will reward you openly" (Matthew 6:17-18).

There are three parts to every man and woman: the flesh, the soul, and the spirit. The flesh is your natural body made from the natural things of earth. The soul is your mind with its thoughts and its feelings, first formed by the Lord in the womb. The spirit is your spiritual being and was born out of heaven. Our original design from heaven was that our spirit would rule over the soul, and then the soul would rule over the flesh. But after the fall everything went upside-down; the flesh became the ruler and the soul became its spokesperson. Every failure of your flesh is supported by your mind and your feelings. When we're born again in the Spirit, we have the foundation for turning things around.

Prayer and fasting aren't just to prepare you for doing a greater work— they are the greater work. "So we fasted and asked our God for this, and he answered our prayer" (Ezra 8:23 CJB).

When I first started fasting, my flesh would run to my soul, who would then try reasoning with me to eat. If that didn't work, my soul would cry and complain, trying to get me to cave in and yield to the desires of my flesh. But as my spirit man grew stronger, I would rebuke my soul to be quiet, and my soul would eventually forfeit. My flesh man became weaker. Going forward, my flesh would simply ask my soul to submit and wait for the fast to be over. Fasting is the exercise that restores the rightful place of your spirit man over your soul, and then your soul over your flesh.

The way you know it's from the flesh is that it feeds the flesh. "Put on the Lord Jesus Christ, and make no provision for the flesh, to gratify its desires" (Romans 13:14 ESV).

You can't believe more until you have more of the Holy Spirit reigning within you. Everything in our natural mind will always battle against the spiritual, supernatural powers of heaven. As long as your faith has its foundation in your own mind—the mind of your soul that's rooted in your flesh—you know nothing of the power of God. You can know everything about Scripture, but until you believe it with the help of the Holy Spirit within you, it's only dead ink on paper to you. But when you believe, when your spirit man is communing with the Holy Spirit of God, your faith can move mountains.

If you can move a mountain with a little faith, just think what you could do with a lot of faith! Jesus taught, "I promise you, if you have faith inside of you no bigger than the size of a small mustard seed, you can say to this mountain, 'Move away from here and go over there,' and you will see it move! There is nothing you couldn't do!" (Matthew 17:20 TPT).

When prison ministry ended for me, I started going to a home church. I experienced some of the most anointed services I've ever been to at that church. On some occasions, I was blessed to give a message there, and other times I was able to minister to some special souls. The services would go from around 6:00 p.m. to midnight or later.

The closer you get to the Lord, the longer you want to stay there.

Stop thinking you need to make time for God, when God created all time for you. "A prophetess named Anna…chose to worship God in the temple continually. For the past eighty-four years she had been serving God with night-and-day prayer and fasting" (Luke 2:36-37 TPT).

One Saturday night, I was on my way to a full evening at this church. I was riding my motorcycle that night and praying as I rode down the freeway. I was very sad on my way there, as I'd eaten some cereal that morning. I'd been fasting for a few days and was famished so decided to eat early that morning, knowing I wouldn't eat until after midnight. But I felt as if I'd betrayed God, because when I fasted for twenty-four hours before ministry, I felt the anointing to do ministry. But this night, I feared I wouldn't be able to.

Too often, we think what God can do through us depends on us.

God can do more with you than your abilities because He fills you with His own. "I have been crucified with Christ: and I myself no longer live, but Christ lives in me. And the real life I now have within this body is a result of my trusting in the Son of God, who loved me and gave himself for me" (Galatians 2:20 TLB).

On my way there, I was pleading with the Lord to forgive me. I just wanted Him to have the right of way in my life so that He could use me. I asked Him to forgive me for not fasting the entire twenty-four hours before ministering, and to still use me that night however He wanted to. I didn't want my failure to take away what God might do for someone else through me. Sometimes our failures are costly to the kingdom.

As I was continuing to ask God to forgive me, I started to get a strong word of conviction. I heard this: *"My power is not dependent on your fasting. The fasting is not for Me but for you, because the fasting prepares you to serve Me."* And then I heard this: *"To show you that I don't need your fasting, you won't even have to speak to others or lay hands on them, but merely breathe on them."* I didn't know what to make of this word. I went to the service and sat quietly by myself the whole time. We must learn to wait patiently for the Lord to reveal to us what He's doing.

Waiting is the hardest thing to do that requires no effort. "My soul, wait silently for God alone, for my expectation is from Him" (Psalm 62:5).

After the service that night, most people left the sanctuary area to go eat and socialize. I remained in the sanctuary area and was sitting in the back. Most of the lights were out, and it was a good time for me to pray in solitude. I didn't want to speak or pray over anyone. I just wanted to be by myself. I always feel so inadequate for ministry, and this night I felt it even more. But a lady there whom I didn't know asked me to pray for her child who wasn't there. It was her teenage daughter who was lost in drugs and living in the world. We need to pray so much for the youth who are getting caught up in the world. We need to pray, believing in all that the Lord can do for them.

Never doubt what God can do if you'll just believe. Jesus promised us, "Yes! I tell you that whoever does not doubt in his heart but trusts that what he says will happen can say to this mountain, 'Go and throw yourself into the sea!' and it will be done for him" (Mark 11:23 CJB).

I prayed with this lady for her daughter. I love to pray for people. It matters so much that we pray for each other. Then she asked me if she could pray for me. I said yes and asked if we could stand. We both stood and faced each other. She laid her hand on my forehead to pray over me, and instantly I collapsed onto the floor. The moment her hand touched my forehead, I felt an overwhelming rush of the Holy Spirit coming over me which literally swept me off my feet. I've experienced this before, so that I can't remain standing. This time I laid there on the floor for a good while. I was so full and complete with His peace.

You can accomplish more in one day filled with the Holy Spirit than a lifetime full of yourself. "Barnabas was a good man, full of the Holy Spirit and strong in faith. And many people were brought to the Lord" (Acts 11:24 NLT).

Eventually I got up, and someone came up to me asking for prayer. It has been my practice to often pray for people with our eyes open and holding hands, so I can look into their spirit through their eyes. Then the Lord will often give me words to say. I'm not sure how that works, but it was what the Holy Spirit had led me to do long before this.

I started to pray for this person, but instead of saying anything or laying my hands on them, I did as the Lord instructed me and simply breathed on their forehead. Instantly this person collapsed to the floor. The Holy Spirit was overwhelming them.

In ministry, we should never think ourselves as something just because we're the utensil God has chosen to use for a time. The violin can't boast in its abilities, but only in its Master.

Live your life so that you're but the violin in the hands of the Master. Then watch as He plays His life song through you onto others. "The LORD will command His lovingkindness in the daytime, and in the night His song shall be with me—A prayer to the God of my life" (Psalm 42:8).

I continued to do this that night, and on some other nights too. It was such a joy to see people immersed in the Holy Spirit. I believed in what God told me, and I acted upon what I believed. That's the faith journey meant for us all—that we would believe upon Him so much that we simply do what He asks us to do.

Whatever it is that you still need to believe in, God is still helping you get there.

In whatever you are facing, trust that God will help you through it. "The Lord also will be a refuge for the oppressed, a refuge in times of trouble. And those who know Your name will put their trust in You; for You, Lord, have not forsaken those who seek You" (Psalm 9:9-10). He's got you.

We mustn't get too wrapped up in mountaintop experiences so that we don't do the real work that's necessary down in the valley. We mustn't chase the spiritual highs and the spiritual gifts, but only receive them as they're needed. My prayer for you is not that you get a particular gift, but that you believe He can give you anything you need. Know that it's not your abilities He's looking for, but your obedience and your willingness. Even when you make a mistake, know that He still loves you and can use you in the kingdom.

Even in your mistakes, God can use you for His glory. "And we know that all things work together for good to those who love God, to those who are the called according to His purpose" (Romans 8:28).

Believe for more, and you'll get more of that which God knows is needed. Oftentimes, what's needed most is that you'll trust in Him alone. Don't ever worry about what talent or gift you lack for serving Him, but only trust Him to give you what you need, when you need it, and to the degree that would bring Him all the glory. Thank Him for only giving you what you're ready for.

Spiritual gifts aren't for you, but are to be through you. "Even so you, since you are zealous for spiritual gifts, let it be for the edification of the church that you seek to excel" (1 Corinthians 14:12).

The Lord won't give you a gift that would puff up your pride and ruin you. If you receive something and think higher of yourself because of it, never be surprised when He takes it back. He only takes from you the thing that would destroy you. The more pride you have, the fewer gifts He'll give you, because He knows they would ruin you. Your humility is the only place that God can rest His gifts upon you. If the gift doesn't point others to Christ, you're headed in the wrong direction.

A plant without roots cannot bear fruit. Never desire the gifts more than the Giver. The Lord Jesus said, "Stay joined to me, and I will stay joined to you. Just as a branch cannot produce fruit unless it stays joined to the vine, you cannot produce fruit unless you stay joined to me" (John 15:4 CEV).

Prayers

* *Heavenly Father, help me to consecrate myself, to set myself apart from the world so I can be joined ever closer to You. Help me be set apart from anything that separates me from You.*

* *Lord Jesus, show me how to be humble in my serving and lowly in my life, so I can serve You rightly. Teach me to live a life of humility.*

* *Holy Spirit, pour into me only that which will bring glory to the Father and honor to the Lord Jesus. Convict me into a life of humble service to the kingdom.*

Spiritual Growth

* **Consecrate yourself:** In prayer, seek the Lord to learn how He would lead you to have a life more consecrated to Himself. Ask Him to show you whatever is in your life that stands between you and Him, and pray for His help in removing it. *The greatest hindrance in your faith is any area of your life not yet nailed upon the cross.* "Then Yeshua said to his disciples, 'Those who want to come with me must say no to the things they want, pick up their crosses, and follow me'" (Matthew 16:24 NOG).

* **Begin fasting:** As far as you're able to safely, set out a plan to begin fasting. And not a one-and-done, but a weekly way of life. To start out, it can be a half-day fast each week. To be an effective fast, it must be a sacrifice and something that's hard for you to do. Learn to let your faith cost you something. Always fast as a sacrifice to God, and not a show before men. *In all you do for the Lord, be sure you do it for Him.* The Lord God said, "When you fasted and mourned... did you really fast for Me—for Me?" (Zechariah 7:5).

* **Be restored:** If you've lost a spiritual gift or have slipped away from your calling, ask Him to show you what needs to change in your life so He can restore you. Don't worry as if you've lost something He can't return. Let yourself be humbled, and trust Him in His timing to restore you. *Never think you can lose a gift from God just because you've strayed too far from Him. You never deserved the gift to begin with. Whenever we're not strong in a gift, be sure we aren't weak before God.* "For the gifts and the calling of God are irrevocable [for He does not withdraw what He has given, nor does He change His mind about those to whom He gives His grace or to whom He sends His call]" (Romans 11:29 AMP).

21

Raising Amelia

*It's not how much you know,
but what you believe.*

"What is faith? It is the confident assurance that something we want is going to happen. It is the certainty that what we hope for is waiting for us, even though we cannot see it up ahead"
(Hebrews 11:1 TLB).

IF YOU CAN BELIEVE God can do anything, there'll be no limit to what you'll pray for here on earth.

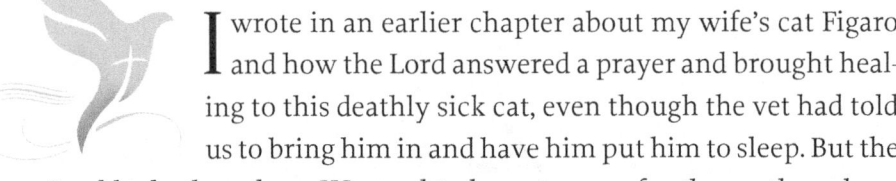

I wrote in an earlier chapter about my wife's cat Figaro and how the Lord answered a prayer and brought healing to this deathly sick cat, even though the vet had told us to bring him in and have him put him to sleep. But the Lord had other plans. We need to learn to pray for these other plans. Figaro was completely healed after prayer, and I've since grown more in my faith, knowing that prayer can heal more than we can even dare to ask for. Never stop praying for the healing of those around you.

The truth of where our faith has flatlined is in those things we've stopped praying for. "One day Jesus told his disciples a story [about the persistent widow] to illustrate their need for constant prayer and to show them that they must keep praying until the answer comes" (Luke 18:1 TLB).

Many years after Figaro was healed, our daughter-in-law's parents had several kittens they were giving away. We were blessed to receive one of them for our youngest daughter. This little kitten was given the name Amelia. She was a pure white kitten with long flowing fur. She was the sweetest little kitten you could ever meet.

Amelia and Figaro became best friends. They had a special bond like we've never seen with Figaro before or ever since. It's such a blessing when there's peace between people and also when there's peace between animals. Peace on earth is a glimpse of what we'll have in heaven.

To have peace on earth, you must focus on heaven. "Wolves will live with lambs. Leopards will lie down with goats. Calves, young lions, and year-old lambs will be together, and little children will lead them" (Isaiah 11:6 NOG).

While Amelia was still young, we scheduled for her to be fixed. We were very concerned, however, because her brother from a previous litter hadn't survived the anesthesia when he was fixed. Her brother's name was Chuck, and he belonged to our son and daughter-in-law. We were all heartbroken when Chuck passed away at such a young age. I can tell a lot about a person by how they feel about animals.

You know the most about a person by the way they treat the least around them. "A good man is concerned for the welfare of his animals" (Proverbs 12:10 TLB).

We let the veterinary staff know about our concerns, and they promised to be very careful with her. Amelia survived the surgery, and we brought her home after it was over. She was having a hard time though, shaking uncontrollably and unable to stand up. My wife Mary and I prayed over her. Then Mary took her into the family room and held her on her lap. I went to work on my writing in my office.

A little later, I heard Mary call out to me, something about Amelia's breathing. I went into the family room, sat next to Mary and laid one hand on Amelia. I remember praying a simple prayer: "Lord, you give us all the breath of life, help our Amelia to breathe, by Your breath Lord, I pray." She looked okay, so I went back to my office. We don't need to be dramatic in our prayers, but just believing. I pray confidently, not because I think my prayers are anything great, but I believe that my prayers are heard by a great God.

Until God says no, keep praying for a yes. Jesus taught us about persistent prayer in this story: "I tell you, even though he will not get up and give him anything just because he is his friend, yet because of his persistence and boldness he will get up and give him whatever he needs" (Luke 11:8 AMP).

Later that evening, Mary came to talk with me. I asked her how Amelia was doing, and to my delight, Amelia was doing great. I was so happy. We have such a wonderful healing Jesus! I asked Mary what had been going on with Amelia's breathing earlier. Mary told me, "Oh, no, you don't understand. She wasn't breathing anymore. She had died."

Friend, would you agree with me that nothing is impossible with God? I don't care how big or difficult the problem is—the Lord can do anything!

Sometimes God makes things impossible for you so you'll know it's only by His power that you can prevail. Jesus prayed, "Abba! Father! You can do anything" (Mark 14:36 NOG).

We need to believe for more each day. We can walk in such a faith that nothing we ask for will seem impossible, as we start to believe on the truth in Scripture that God can do anything. It's the most incredible place to be when once you believe what the Lord can really do. It takes no effort at all to get there, but only one prayer—that your Father would help you.

Believing more is about letting go more, and trusting in your Father.

The reason so few grow into a mighty faith is that they try to do it on their own power. "And the apostles said to the Lord, 'Increase our faith'" (Luke 17:5).

Even when we have all the faith in what the Lord can do, sometimes He doesn't do as we hoped He would. A few years after Amelia was raised from the dead, she'd grown to nearly full size. It turned out she was completely deaf. She would respond only if she saw you or felt you. Even in our flaws, God's perfect design is extraordinary. We adored Amelia, and she was a special part of our family.

There was a time when Amelia became very sick. We prayed for her healing, but she wasn't getting any better. Her breathing became so shallow that we took her to the vet to be checked. They had us take her to the animal hospital so they could treat her with oxygen. A few hours later, we got a call from the hospital. Amelia had died.

Time seems to stop when death knocks on the door. I'll never forget hearing my wife give this news to our daughter. We were all so sad to lose Amelia.

Though God may be silent for a time, yet He still hears your every cry. "In my distress I called upon the Lord, and cried out to my God; He heard my voice from His temple, and my cry entered His ears" (2 Samuel 22:7).

I don't know why the Lord would raise her from the dead and then allow her to die a few years later. I believe God can always heal, whether He chooses to or not. Our place is to pray for the healing, and to trust Him with the outcome. In the miracles, your faith is stirred up, but it's in the worst of times that the roots of your faith are forced to burrow down deeper. The Father doesn't have to explain Himself to His children.

The higher you want to grow in your faith, the deeper the roots must go. "His delight is in the law of the Lord, and in His law he meditates day and night. He shall be like a tree planted by the rivers of water, that brings forth its fruit in its season, whose leaf also shall not wither; and whatever he does shall prosper" (Psalm 1:2-3).

A few months after this, I was getting ready to head out to Boston. I was still in the job commuting from Los Angeles to Boston almost every week. Our dog Simone was getting up there at fifteen years old, but still getting around pretty well. The day before I was to leave for Boston, she wasn't eating, so I brought her into my office to pray for her. Throughout the day she got worse and was staggering around, unable to walk very well. She looked so frightened, not knowing what was happening.

I took her to the vet with my wife, and we learned that her liver was failing. They showed us that her eyes had a yellow tint. We had to put her to sleep right there. I held her in my arms when they gave her the shot. I was petting her and telling her everything was going to be okay. And then she died. Death is such a tragedy. I look forward to heaven when it will not happen anymore. I've lost family, friends, and many of my animals, and it's so hard to say goodbye.

Don't let hard times harden you. God will listen to those with tender hearts. "Because your heart was tender, and you humbled yourself before the Lord...and wept before Me, I also have heard you, says the Lord" (2 Kings 22:19).

There are some chapters in our lives that end badly. When that happens, we need to learn how to thank the Lord for all He gave us, and to trust Him in those things we no longer have. Some things happen to us that we'll likely never understand this side of heaven. Those things will either cause you to trust the Lord more or to trust the Lord less. The choice you make in trusting God depends on whether you'll accept His silence when you ask Him to explain what He's doing. Learn the lesson of His silence, which is to trust Him even when you don't understand Him.

Even in His silence, He's teaching you a lesson. "Without faith it is impossible to please Him, for he who comes to God must believe that He is, and that He is a rewarder of those who diligently seek Him" (Hebrews 11:6).

It's true that we must believe to receive. But there's a higher truth: We must believe whether or not we receive. Grieve for what you've lost, and give thanks for all that the Lord has given you. You have to walk through the wilderness to get to the promise. When you're going through the hard times, just know that He's with you and there's something good that lies ahead, even if you have to wait until you get to heaven to receive it. Someday it may be an unanswered prayer that will get you into heaven.

The closer you get to heaven, the less you worry about the things of this world. "We are looking forward to God's promise of new heavens and a new earth afterwards, where there will be only goodness" (2 Peter 3:13 TLB).

Prayers

- *Heavenly Father, help me pray with the faith that You can do all things, and help me trust You whether or not You do the things I pray for.*

- *Lord Jesus, help me trust You even in the things I cannot understand. Help me reach that higher faith where I believe, whether or not I receive.*

- *Holy Spirit, guide me to continue faithfully in prayer even when there are unanswered prayers behind me. Teach me to never give up in my prayers.*

Spiritual Growth

* **Pray for more faith:** Whatever level you're at as a believer, pray to believe more. Faith is meant to be alive and growing. Believing should be like a river that never stops flowing. *Faith doesn't grow from knowing more but from believing more. The measure of your faith is the height of your prayers when nobody's watching. Pray as big as God is. We pray to the degree that we believe.* Jesus promised, "And whatever you ask for in prayer, having faith and [really] believing, you will receive" (Matthew 21:22 AMPC).

* **Keep knocking:** When your prayers aren't answered right away, just keep praying. Some prayers just take more time. Until God clearly answers no, keep praying for a yes. Sometimes the delay is simply there to test your faith. *You'll have a stronger faith when you exercise your faith.* Jesus taught us, "Ask, and it will be given to you; seek, and you will find; knock, and it will be opened to you" (Matthew 7:7).

* **Grieve righteously:** Don't hide your sorrow from the Lord. Just tell Him how you feel. He already knows your heart, but you bless Him when you trust Him with it. Know that in all suffering, He's with you and able to help you along the way. *God's comfort is not so you'll get over it, but so that you'll get through it.* "Blessed be the God and Father of our Lord Jesus Christ, the Father of mercies and God of all comfort, who comforts us in all our tribulation" (2 Corinthians 1:3-4).

22

Pray Like You Mean It

If you want to avail much, you have to travail much.

"The effectual fervent prayer of a righteous man availeth much" (James 5:16 KJV).

IF YOU CAN BELIEVE the Lord is moved by your fervent prayers, you'll become even more fervent in the things you pray for.

We can learn so much about prayer and how we might make our requests known to God. We can learn a certain process in which we come before God. But what makes prayer so powerful is not in the process but in our passion. The process we follow proves the obedience in our actions, but our passion proves the devotion we have in our heart. God honors our process, but He longs for our passion.

Your emotions are the rivers that pour out from your heart. The deeper the heart, the stronger the river. "Pour out your heart like water before the face of the Lord" (Lamentations 2:19).

If you want to reach the Father's heart in your prayers, you must do that from your own heart. When we pray from our innermost feelings, we skip right past the process and dive deep into our emotions, from which we can then move God.

Never think God is more interested in the mechanics of your prayer than in the surrendered heart your prayer flows from. It's when we're closest with the Father that we can cry out to Him as His child, and we'll know that He hears us and loves us with a Father's heart.

Prayer is the path between God's heart and yours. "Then you will call upon Me, and you will come and pray to Me, and I will hear and heed you. Then you will seek Me, inquire for, and require Me [as a vital necessity] and find Me when you search for Me with all your heart" (Jeremiah 29:12-13 AMPC).

The Lord uses circumstances to teach us lessons. Some of His deepest lessons are born out of our sorrows. My family was still very sad from losing my daughter's cat Amelia and our dog Simone. In my house, pets are like family, and when we lose one, we grieve. You can tell a lot about a person's heart in how they're connected to God's creatures. I think that if you care two cents about God, you'll respect and honor all His creation.

A few weeks after we lost these two pets, our cat Figaro became terribly sick again, and wasn't eating at all. He's the cat the Lord brought healing to, many years before. We prayed over him again, but this time he wasn't being healed by the Lord. We took him to the vet to see what was wrong with him. They gave him some treatments, but he still wasn't getting better. He was shrinking away, losing weight, and just lying around all the time and not eating.

I know all things come to an end. All God's children and all His creatures will someday pass away. But had I fallen into error somewhere without realizing it? I didn't understand. It's okay for us to feel that way. God is so much higher than us that we must never pretend we have Him and His plans all figured out. King David cried out a hundred questions to the Lord in the Psalms. Let us be willing to do the same. Stop trying to appear so high in your faith, and just go to the Lord with your questions.

In the kingdom, your stature is determined by how low you'll kneel. "Humble yourselves [feeling very insignificant] in the presence of the Lord, and He will exalt you [He will lift you up and make your lives significant]" (James 4:10 AMPC).

I cried out to the Lord to help me know what to do. That's when the Spirit revealed to me: *"You need to pray like you mean it."* That really affected me, because I'm not one to pray with a lot of passion. I'd been praying with belief and in righteousness, but not with fervency. Immediately the Spirit brought to my mind this verse: "The effective, fervent prayer of a righteous man avails much" (James 5:16). It's not enough to be righteous—we must be fervent in our prayers.

Being persistent in prayer means to never stop until you get what you're praying for. "So Peter was kept in prison, but fervent and persistent prayer for him was being made to God by the church" (Acts 12:5 AMP).

I repented before the Lord. I wanted to live a life of fervent praying.

Friend, stop thinking you're beyond repenting. We always have something to repent from. Repenting is not a one-time act, but an ever growing process of letting go of all that doesn't belong. Sin isn't just doing wrong; it's missing the mark—failing to hit the bull's-eye with every action we do, every word we speak, every thought we have, and every prayer we say to the Lord.

Repenting isn't just being sorry for what you did but being determined for what you'll do next. "All must repent of their sins and turn to God—and prove they have changed by the good things they do" (Acts 26:20 NLT).

That afternoon, I was alone at home with Figaro. I went up next to him. We'd just lost two pets and were about to lose a third. And Figaro is so special to me—God's little miracle on paws. I got down on the ground next to the chair he was lying on. I sat there cross-legged and started to pray. I was thanking the Lord for His great mercy on my life. I was praising Him for all the miracles He has allowed me to see. Then I started to pray for Figaro. I prayed in the Spirit for some time. I'd just lost two animals, and I knew that Figaro was looking really bad. But I just kept believing enough to keep praying.

God knows when we aren't willing to give up for the thing we're praying for. Pray like that, and you'll be a blessing for the kingdom.

Believe that you can have something, and you just might get it. "And we are confident that he hears us whenever we ask for anything that pleases him. And since we know he hears us when we make our requests, we also know that he will give us what we ask for" (1 John 5:14-15 NLT).

When I was done, I went to my office, and I was thanking the Lord for the anointed time He allowed me to have with Him. I thanked him for the conviction to pray fervently.

Friend, learn to love the convictions, as they're the sign God knows you're ready to change and go higher. I was praying that my earlier prayer had been an acceptable fragrance to the Lord. Then I got a convicting word from the Lord: *"Why don't you pray for My children like that?"* That conviction really stung me. It changed the direction of my prayer life from that day forward. How lightly we often take our responsibility for intercessory prayer for others.

So long as you're convicted of the Holy Spirit, you're on the right track. Jesus promised us, "When He, the Spirit of truth, has come, He will guide you into all truth" (John 16:13).

A few minutes after the Lord had convicted me with the word, *"Why don't you pray for My children like that?"* I got a phone call. It was from Carol Ann Waisanen, a pastor. I'd met her briefly several weeks earlier at the church where she and her husband pastored. I'd been instantly drawn to her kindness and her spirit. I'd gone to that church to see a young lady I know preach her first sermon. I'd spoken with Pastor Carol Ann for a short time after that service, and I gave her my contact information, but I never really expected to hear from her. But I was so glad to hear from her, as she had seemed so genuine when I'd first met her.

If you want to be special—just be yourself, because there's none other made the same as you. "He fashions their hearts individually; He considers all their works" (Psalm 33:15).

After Pastor Carol Ann greeted me over the phone, right away she asked when I could come to her church and preach on healing. I'd just been rocked with not understanding why the Lord wasn't answering my prayers on healing, and here a pastor I barely knew was asking me to come preach on healing at her church.

Friend, nothing happens by accident with an all-powerful and all-knowing Lord. God had broken open the ground of my faith so He could then grow something from it. Never underestimate the purposes of God formed in the circumstances of your life.

Don't worry as if God is not sovereign. "The LORD of Heaven's Armies has sworn this oath: 'It will all happen as I have planned. It will be as I have decided'" (Isaiah 14:24 NLT).

Pastor Carol Ann spoke with me for a long time. I'm so blessed by those special souls God has placed in my path. She spent much time speaking about the great healer, Smith Wigglesworth. I've come to admire the writings from Wigglesworth and the boldness of his preaching. We need more preaching like his that goes after the things of the Lord with fervency and passion. Some of the stories from Wigglesworth involved praying all night and sometimes for several days in a row until the prayer was answered. How much we all need to learn to pray with a greater fervency and a higher faith.

God wants you to graduate to higher levels of believing. Jesus taught, "You can pray for anything, and if you have faith, you will receive it" (Matthew 21:22 NLT).

I've come to find in my life the weaving of the Lord in how things come together. I've learned that the circumstances I go through, the people He puts in my path, and the words I hear from the Holy Spirit are all working together for God's purposes. We're meant to live a life of intimacy with the Lord. We're meant to have divine encounters and spiritual lessons that grow us toward the purposes of heaven. When we're kingdom-minded, we'll be kingdom-focused and looking for how our Father is working in our lives and the lives of those around us.

If you want God to touch other people through you, you must first be touched by God.

Touching the deep things of God requires that first God has touched the deep things in you. "Deep calls unto deep at the noise of Your waterfalls; all Your waves and billows have gone over me" (Psalm 42:7).

The Lord answered my prayer for Figaro. He was healed, and to this day, many years later, he's still doing great. He's as skinny as a living cat can be, but he's alive. I prayed the prayer of Hezekiah over him that the Lord will extend his life fifteen years. We'll see how that goes. What I know is that I learned how much I need to pray for God's children—for the sick, for the dying, and even for the dead to be raised, if this is in His will. And not only to pray for them, but to pray *fervently* for them.

Selfless prayers are the purest requests made known to God. "So we have not stopped praying for you since we first heard about you. We ask God to give you complete knowledge of his will and to give you spiritual wisdom and understanding" (Colossians 1:9 NLT).

My prayer for you is that you'll learn to pray like you mean it. Pray in the Spirit. Be so filled with the Spirit of God that there's no room left for your tears to remain inside you. Let the Holy Spirit have His way with you. You'll never go wrong with this advice. The Father sent the Holy Spirit to live within you, and He wants you to know you're never alone. You can pray in the Spirit because the Spirit is in you. Pray until the tears begin to flow. Pray with a fervency that makes the demons flee and the angels sing around you. Pray like you mean it.

Once you begin to pray in the Holy Spirit, natural prayers will have no place in your life. "But you, dear friends, must build each other up in your most holy faith, pray in the power of the Holy Spirit" (Jude 1:20 NLT).

Prayers

* *Heavenly Father, I know Your power doesn't depend on my prayers, yet You choose to use prayer as the path Your power flows through. Help me to pray more fervently.*

* *Lord Jesus, I want to experience Your life in me as I'm praying, so that my prayers are founded on a higher faith, with a richer depth of Your precious love upon them.*

* *Holy Spirit, reveal to me and guide me into a faith that grows nearer to heaven with every breath I take. Help me pray fervently for my Father's children.*

Spiritual Growth

* **Pray for others:** Spend most of your prayer time praying for others. Ask people what they need prayer for. They don't have to believe—but you do. Be willing to sacrifice a little time in order to win a person's soul to the Lord for all eternity. *If you pray only for yourself, that says much about you. How off we can be that even in our prayers to God we could be so selfish!* "First of all, then, I urge that petitions (specific requests), prayers, intercessions (prayers for others) and thanksgivings be offered on behalf of all people" (1 Timothy 2:1 AMP).

* **Pray with faith:** Your prayer life reflects the level of your faith. The more you believe, the more you'll pray for. We must never think the test of our prayers is in whether they're answered, because the only test of our prayers is whether we have the faith to pray them. Have faith in God, and let the outcomes be His concern. *The same Holy Spirit that dwelt in Peter dwells in you.* "They even carried their sick out into the streets and put them on cots and sleeping pads, so that when Peter came by at least his shadow might fall on one of them [with healing power]" (Acts 5:15 AMP).

* **Pray fervently:** In your faith journey, becoming an intercessor who prays fervently for others will be one of the greatest blessings you can do for the kingdom. We see many people trying to make a name for themselves in ministry, but its that unknown person praying in the backroom who has the ear of God. Be that person. *If you really want to change someone, pray for them.* "Epaphras, who is one of you, a bondservant of Christ, greets you, always laboring fervently for you in prayers, that you may stand perfect and complete in all the will of God" (Colossians 4:12).

23

Plans of God

In your prayers, don't try to lower the Lord into your plans, but ask Him to raise you into His.

"The Lord Yahweh, Commander of Angel Armies, makes this solemn decree: 'Be sure of this: Just as I have planned, so it will be. Every purpose of my heart will surely come to pass'"
(Isaiah 14:24 TPT).

IF YOU CAN BELIEVE God's plans for your life are better than your plans, you'll trust Him with His leading.

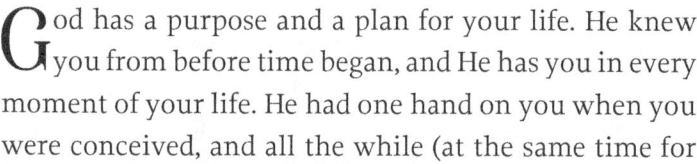

God has a purpose and a plan for your life. He knew you from before time began, and He has you in every moment of your life. He had one hand on you when you were conceived, and all the while (at the same time for Him) His other hand is holding you as you step into heaven. He has you in the good times and in the bad. The Lord has used every difficulty you've been through to change you. In every circumstance you're in now, He's using it to form you. He has a purpose for every suffering, and there's value in every tear.

Though you may not understand Him, you can trust Him in everything that you're going through.

Don't fear what's ahead; just trust Him to get you through it. "You will not leave in a hurry, running for your lives. For the LORD will go ahead of you; yes, the God of Israel will protect you from behind" (Isaiah 52:12 NLT).

In every trial, we need to believe God has us. We need to trust that God is using everything to shape us into something new. If we believe nothing's impossible for God, we'll realize that God can change us into something new no matter how messed up we may think we are. No matter how dark your past, His light can yet shine brightly in you. No matter how deep your wounds, the Lord can yet heal you. No matter how deficient you may be for serving Him, He can yet provide everything you need. Believe God can help you, and He will.

In whatever you're battling, if you turn to God, He will help you. "Do not fear, for I am with you; do not anxiously look about you, for I am your God. I will strengthen you, surely I will help you, surely I will uphold you with My righteous right hand" (Isaiah 41:10 NASB).

After I found out that my current job was coming to an end, I began to search for a new job. I've found that when the Lord wants to test my faith most, He places me in circumstances where I must believe Him the most. I spent some months looking for a job, believing that God would help me. I wasn't making any progress at all. Finally, I ended up finding a job in an industry I was experienced in, and it was located near where I lived. It seemed like the perfect job. I had several interviews, and everything was going great. It felt like I was stepping into a season of blessings in all that my Father was doing for me.

To realize your blessings, just try to count them. "Many, O LORD my God, are Your wonderful works which You have done; and Your thoughts toward us cannot be recounted to You in order; if I would declare and speak of them, they are more than can be numbered" (Psalm 40:5).

On my final interview, I was going to meet with the man who'd be my boss. We were both traveling at the time, so we just met over the phone. Before I spoke with him, I prayed to the Lord that if this was the right job, this man wouldn't even ask me a question but simply hire me. When I called him, he answered and right away he said to me, "I don't even need to ask you anything, I can see that you're right for this job. If you want it, then it's yours." Sometimes God's answers to prayers are so overwhelming I can hardly sit still.

God knows the answer before the problem. "For your Father knows the things you have need of before you ask Him" (Matthew 6:8).

This was happening at just the perfect time, as I was scheduled to go to a large event at my current company that was already planning to get rid of me. It was going to be a time of humiliation in that I was going to be paraded about in my reduced role in the company. As much as we might think ourselves not prideful, we are.

If you're truly humble, nobody can hurt your pride. "A person's pride will humiliate him, but a humble spirit gains honor" (Proverbs 29:23 NOG).

A few weeks later I traveled to Ohio. While there, I got an email from the human resources person at the new company I was applying to. She wanted to arrange for a call. I had a bad feeling. I went to my hotel room and called her. She told me that there was a problem and they wouldn't be able to hire me. The division I was getting hired into had financial difficulties, and the corporate leadership had mandated no new hires for them. I was crushed. I was so sure that the Lord had given this job to me, and now it was gone. Now I'd have to endure the humiliation at the event for my current job. I wondered why God had allowed this to happen to me.

The hardest truth is when you know God can do anything, but He chooses not to. "Why are you far away, Lord? Why do you hide yourself when I am in trouble?" (Psalm 10:1 CEV).

That evening I went out to a church in Ohio called Heart Afire. I'd found this church earlier while traveling to Ohio, and whenever I was in the area I would go there. We always need to look for fellowship with other believers wherever we go. There will be times in our lives when we find out just how valuable fellowship can be in helping us through the hardest of times. I believe God allowed me to be crushed on the very day that I could go out to this church. I was so blessed when I went there that night, but I kept my troubles to myself. When I came back to my hotel room, I was still crushed. I sat for some time that night on the floor in prayer. Sometimes I don't even know what to pray for.

God has to crush your life out of you to put His life into you—"that you may be filled to the measure of all the fullness of God" (Ephesians 3:19 NIV).

The next morning, I awoke and started my day as I always do. I prayed, read a devotion, and wrote in my journal. Then I waited on the Holy Spirit to give me a word to write for the day. I've been doing this for many years, pressing in to hear the Lord and then posting it online. But I heard nothing. I felt like I was abandoned by God. I was even more crushed, wondering why He was doing this to me. The hardest time to understand the Lord is when He doesn't make any sense to you. I know that He's a good Father, but sometimes He gives hard lessons.

The Lord prunes more so that you can be more. Jesus taught, "Every branch that bears fruit He prunes, that it may bear more fruit" (John 15:2).

I waited and waited on God, and all I heard was silence. I'd made it my ministry in posting these words from the Holy Spirit for many years. I was busy writing blogs and preparing to write books using some of these words. It felt like it was over.

Finally, I had to leave for the airport. I sat down and prayed one more time. When you're truly surrendered to the Lord, you're willing to accept His answer, even if His answer doesn't make sense to you.

The evidence of a life that has surrendered all is a life that has nothing to lose. Be the Joshua in this generation, the person who can say, "My brothers (fellow spies) who went up with me made the heart of the people melt with fear; but I followed the Lord my God completely" (Joshua 14:8 AMP).

I remember telling God that I couldn't fake it—that if the flowing from the Holy Spirit was stopped, then I wouldn't write as if it was still flowing. I'd rather end my writing ministry in truth than continue it in a lie. Though I can be clever on occasion, I just can't pretend to say a thing if it isn't true. We dare not slander a mighty God and expect Him not to judge us. I was committed to keeping it real, even if it meant my ministry would be over. We serve Him at His pleasure, not ours.

Whatever your problem, just give it to the Lord, and you can be sure it's in good hands. "For I, the Lord your God, will hold your right hand, saying to you, 'Fear not, I will help you'" (Isaiah 41:13).

My first flight that day was from Cleveland to Chicago. I was resigned that the Lord was ending my writing ministry before it ever really took off. The Lord had ended prison ministry for me a few years earlier, and so I knew that my service to Him is at His pleasure, not mine. When I got to Chicago, I was sitting in the airport waiting for the next flight. As I sat there in prayer, resigned to whatever the Lord had for me, I got a word from the Holy Spirit and posted it soon after. I heard these words: *"When you wrestle with God, He will always win."*

You have to wrestle with God to get the blessing. Faith is always active, whereas doubt will never move. "Then Jacob was left alone; and a Man [the Lord] wrestled with him until the breaking of day. Now when He saw that He did not prevail against him...He said, 'Let Me go, for the day breaks.' But he [Jacob] said, 'I will not let You go unless You bless me!'" (Genesis 32:24-26). *Grab hold of God, and never let go.*

I boarded my flight to go back home. Usually, on these longer flights, I'd read my Bible or do some writing. But I was still not in the right spirit to do anything. I was still crushed. I'd been so sure that my Father was rescuing me—then it felt like it was Him who threw me out into the sea. I was dreading the humility that would soon come upon me at my current job. I needed an escape on this flight, and I had nowhere I could go. Finally, I picked up a book I'd been reading called *Humility*, written by Andrew Murray. I opened to read the next chapter from where I'd last left off. By the sovereign plans of God, it was a chapter entitled "Humility and Death to Self."

The more humble you are, the more He can exalt you. "And whoever exalts himself will be humbled, and he who humbles himself will be exalted" (Matthew 23:12).

As I read the words from this chapter, I knew that the Lord had arranged this moment. Every word in this chapter ministered to me. The words brought the truth of the value in having humiliation crush you like a grape and prepare you for all that God would have you be. Murray wrote of how great it was when others humiliate you, because this helps you to be more humble, and thus more useful in the hands of God. He went on to expound on the great benefits to a believer who, through humility, has died to self and been made right with God.

You have to crush the grape to make the wine. "Count it all joy when you fall into various trials, knowing that the testing of your faith produces [those things God wants to form in you]" (James 1:2-3).

I'm confident that God was testing me that day on whether I would keep it real with my ministry. I'm also sure that the Lord was forming humility in me so that He could use me in new ways. I've learned that the things that crush our flesh are the very things that strengthen our spirit.

You can be sure that in every difficult circumstance, the Lord is busy at work in how it will form you into something new. It's a kingdom principle that something must be broken before God can form it into something new.

When God crushes you, and still you trust Him, then you're walking on kingdom ground. "Though he slay me, I will hope in him" (Job 13:15 ESV).

In whatever you're going through, and in however you feel crushed by your circumstances, know that your Father loves you and has a plan for you. There's nothing He doesn't know, and there's nothing He can't do to help you in everything you're going through. Learn to let humility change you into all that the Lord has ordained for you to become. You must go through the difficulties on level one before you'll be prepared to endure what lies ahead on level two.

Humility is the window to see what needs to change in you. "The humble He teaches His way" (Psalm 25:9).

Believe that God is shaping you in all that you're going through. Trust that He can use you in your weakness and lift you up from the place where you find yourself right now. Believe that your Father loves you even when it seems as though He doesn't. Believe that the Lord has a plan for you, and trust Him that He has you. Place your faith on the One who is forming you.

If you can believe God can change you—He will. The Lord Jesus promised us, "Everything is possible for one who believes" (Mark 9:23 NIV).

Prayers

* *Heavenly Father, help me to know that You're with me in the good times and in the bad times. Help me to trust You in the bad times, and not to squander what You're forming in me.*

* *Lord Jesus, help me keep my eyes on You, so that Your peace remains on me. Help me to know that You're with me even when it seems as though You're not.*

✣ *Holy Spirit, pour into me a greater measure, so that I may learn and follow as you teach and guide me in everything I should say and do. Help me to serve Jesus faithfully.*

Spiritual Growth

✣ **Let Him form you:** In whatever way you're feeling crushed in your life right now, pray to the Lord that He'll use it to form you into something new. Don't allow bitterness to get in the way of the righteousness that God is forming in you. *The power of God to change you lies in your belief that He can.* "The vessel that he was making of clay was spoiled in the hand of the potter; so he remade it into another vessel, as it pleased the potter to make" (Jeremiah 18:4 NASB).

✣ **Trust His plan:** Determine in your heart that you'll trust in the Lord even when you don't understand Him. Trusting Him more will be one of the greatest changes to help you grow in your faith. The Lord has to test your faith to grow your faith, so trust Him in the testing. Profess your trust in the midst of the unknown. *Anybody can praise God in the good times, but it's the blessed ones who can praise Him in the bad times.* "Even when it seems I'm surrounded by many liars and my own fears, and though I'm hurting in my suffering and trauma, I still stay faithful to God and speak words of faith" (Psalm 116:10-11 TPT).

✣ **Be humble:** God will place people in your path and use them to teach you a lesson. Often the lesson will be to show you where pride still reigns inside you. Instead of getting angry when someone hurts your pride, be thankful that they showed it to you. If you want to grow in your faith, your pride will have to go. *It's hard to humiliate someone walking in humility.* "Before being ruined, a person's heart is proud; before being honored, a person must be humble" (Proverbs 18:12 CJB).

24

All Things are Possible

God can't meet you at the point of impossibility unless you believe in Him enough to go meet Him there.

"For with God nothing [is or ever] shall be impossible"
(Luke 1:37 AMP).

IF YOU CAN BELIEVE that nothing's impossible for God, then in your prayers you'll ask for the impossible with the confidence that He can do it.

Sometimes we can't understand a thing until it's behind us. When we look back, we gain a perspective and begin to understand the things that the Lord was doing. When we learn to see all that He has done, our faith will grow, and our confidence will be elevated. As we believe more, we'll find more of God's power unleashed around us. This is the plan of God—that our faith would grow, and we would learn just how much we can trust Him.

The maturity of a Christian is measured not in years, but by their faith. "And now, just as you accepted Christ Jesus as your Lord, you must continue to follow him. Let your roots grow down into him, and let your lives be built on him. Then your faith will grow strong in the truth you were taught, and you will overflow with thankfulness" (Colossians 2:6-7 NLT).

One of the biggest things we learn as we grow in our faith is just how powerful our God is. Nothing is impossible for Him, whether it be something grand or something very small. When we start to discern the moves of the Lord around us, we find just how intimately He's working in our lives. Where we once longed to see some great miracle, we've grown to be in awe of all the small things the Lord arranges in our lives each day. Learn to see God in every circumstance and trust Him with all He's doing.

Believe that God can do anything, and trust that He will do the right thing. "He is the Rock, His work is perfect; for all His ways are justice, a God of truth and without injustice; righteous and upright is He" (Deuteronomy 32:4).

I ended up getting a new job, and it has turned out well for me. The companies where I was before, as well as the company where I didn't get the job, have not done well at all. It often happens this way, that the thing we thought we were losing was something God was rescuing us from. When we believe that our Father can provide for us, we can rest in all His promises.

Don't worry as if your Father has forgotten you. Take solace in knowing He will never let go of you, and His plans for you will never fail.

When the Lord has you go through something difficult, it's often to save you from something worse. Joseph told his brothers who had sold him into slavery, "You meant to do me harm, but God meant it for good—so that it would come about as it is today, with many people's lives being saved" (Genesis 50:20 CJB).

This new job I got didn't require me to travel, so it gave me more time to devote to my writing ministry. When we're obedient to the leading of the Lord, we can always trust in where He's taking us. This doesn't mean that our journey will be easy, but that it will be in the will of God. When we believe that He can lead us—He will.

Be patient until He leads you. You'll never regret waiting on the Lord. Learn to trust Him in your season of waiting.

Resting in Him exercises your faith. "I stand silently before the LORD, waiting for him to rescue me. For salvation comes from him alone" (Psalm 62:1 TLB).

There are some things that the Lord has never healed me from. We mustn't think that He leaves us in a condition for no reason. There's nothing the Lord allows or does for which there isn't a reason. Don't ever squander all that suffering can bring you.

When I began to flow in hearing the Holy Spirit every morning, this was my first prayer and the first words I received: *Father God, I know that every tear produced in suffering is not wasted in Your kingdom. Tears water the life so it can produce fruit. Every suffering has a purpose.* "You've kept track of all my wandering and my weeping. You've stored my many tears in your bottle—not one will be lost. For they are all recorded in your book of remembrance" (Psalm 56:8 TPT).

We think that our life should be like a fairy tale with every ending a happily-ever-after. But God has higher purposes for you than to reach the end of your faith journey. We think we should get to a place where we're satisfied—but He's taking us to a place to make us more. We want to get to the place we want, but He's taking us to a place we need to get to. Be sure that His plan for you is better than yours. He often uses suffering in one thing to heal us from another. Don't put God into a box in how He might change you.

Just when you think you know how God will do things, He will choose another way. "For as the heavens are higher than the earth, so are My ways higher than your ways, and My thoughts than your thoughts" (Isaiah 55:9).

I continue to pray for healing in the lives of people around me. Sometimes God does such a great miracle, and other times He will not. But I have faith that He can do anything, and I believe in what He can do, whether He does it or not. As you go along in your faith journey and you believe more, then you'll receive more, for this is a principle born out of heaven. But when you don't receive more, you can still believe for the more when your faith outweighs the things that stand before you. Believe for more, and let God decide on the outcomes.

Faith is the doorway through which the power of God will flow. It's not enough to pray for healing, but you must believe. "So Abraham prayed to God; and God healed Abimelech, his wife, and his female servants. Then they bore children" (Genesis 20:17).

It was sad for me to leave prison ministry and then to stop preaching at an outside church the year after that. I dearly miss ministering to people in person. I miss having times of fellowship. God has me locked away in solitude. Yet I've seen the fruit of God's leading me to be set apart and to write for the kingdom. Our obedience matters to the kingdom.

Consider the loss for the kingdom because of the things you hold onto in your life. "Therefore we also, since we are surrounded by so great a cloud of witnesses, let us lay aside every weight, and the sin which so easily ensnares us, and let us run with endurance the race that is set before us" (Hebrews 12:1).

Life is not easy. It seems that when we solve one problem, a new one is soon to follow. We can get consumed in what's wrong and become bitter. We can become overwhelmed by all we face and lose hope. But the Father wants His children to operate at a different level, one of total trust in all that He can do. When it seems like there's nothing you can do, there is—believe in Him. If you can believe, then your life will be His instrument.

In the kingdom, having faith is more important than having the things our faith is hoping for. "Faith makes us sure of what we hope for and gives us proof of what we cannot see" (Hebrews 11:1 CEV).

Where is it that you need to believe for more? What challenges do you face that require you to have more faith? When once you see your circumstances as the lesson and trust that the Lord can help you through them, everything will change for you. God can change you. He can turn your life around and make you a new creature. All it takes is believing He can—then you let Him do it.

You'll be surprised what God can do in your life if only you let Him. "And I pray that he would unveil within you the unlimited riches of his glory and favor until supernatural strength floods your innermost being with his divine might and explosive power. Then, by constantly using your faith, the life of Christ will be released deep inside you" (Ephesians 3:16-17 TPT).

There are some things we pray for that seem impossible in the eyes of men. The more impossible it is, the more we need to have faith in a God who can do anything. When you can believe to that level, nothing will seem too high to pray for. There are people in your life who'll be forever blessed when you believe more, because your prayers for them will carry weight and bring heaven's favor down upon them.

Impossible situations demand our God, through whom everything is possible. Jesus taught us, "The things which are impossible with men are possible with God" (Luke 18:27).

When we pray to our Father, we must have faith that nothing's impossible for Him. Our confidence in Him is to be founded not on how He might answer our prayers, but on the truth in God's Word that He can do anything. When you believe with all your heart that God can do anything, there won't be a storm big enough to rock you out of the boat.

Sometimes God puts you in a storm so that you can preach on His protection. "He calms the storm, so that its waves are still" (Psalm 107:29).

There are seasons in our lives where so much is going wrong, and so little seems to make sense. It's in the hardest of times where our faith is tested most. When I pray, I repeat back to God the promises of the truth in His Word—that nothing is impossible for Him. He knows this already, but saying it brings me confidence as I pray. There's no greater thing we can do than to pray over others with the confidence born out of heaven of the truth in God's Word that all things are possible—and no prayer request is too hard for God.

A believing prayer warrior is a dangerous thing in the midst of an evil world. Jesus promised, "Listen to the truth I speak to you: Whoever says to this mountain with great faith and does not doubt, 'Mountain, be lifted up and thrown into the midst of the sea,' and believes that what he says will happen, it will be done" (Mark 11:23 TPT).

I'm convinced that we shortchange our prayer requests by not thinking our Father can or will answer them. We're better at rationalizing away what He won't do than we are at realizing all He can do. Just pray for the impossible, and leave the answer up to God. Don't worry about what people think of you. Everyone thought Noah was crazy, and look at what this got them. Just believe God can do all things, and you'll be aligned with the truth found in heaven.

If you want to know where you lack faith, it's what you think is impossible for God to do. Jeremiah said, "Ah, Lord God! Behold, You have made the heavens and the earth by Your great power and outstretched arm. There is nothing too hard for You" (Jeremiah 32:17).

The more impossible your prayer, the less you can doubt the power of God when He answers it. Consider all that the Lord might put before you to see how much you might dare to believe in all that He can do. The more you trust in God, the easier it is to pray for the impossible. I believe that our Father places impossible things before us to see if we will dare to pray that He would solve them. If you believe God can do anything, you'll pray that He'll do it.

Be the one in your circle of influence who believes for the impossible. Jesus said, "I can promise you this. If you had faith no larger than a mustard seed, you could tell this mountain to move from here to there. And it would. Everything would be possible for you" (Matthew 17:20 CEV).

It's not enough to pray for the impossible; you must *believe* that there's nothing impossible for God. Believing is trusting, and trusting is acknowledging the power and majesty of God. You open a door believing you can walk through it. Pray with the same sense of confidence in what the Lord can do.

How much you believe is how confident you are. Jesus said, "For this reason I am telling you, whatever things you ask for in prayer [in accordance with God's will], believe [with confident trust] that you have received them, and they will be given to you" (Mark 11:24 AMP).

We think it's the specific answer to a prayer that's most important. But what matters most is not what God would do, but what you're willing to trust Him with. Your Father has you for all eternity, so why are you worrying about a couple of days here on earth? Trust that He has you in your couple of days here on earth. No matter the storm that's before you, believe that He can calm it. Whatever it is that you're lacking in life, just know that He can fill it. Believe Him for what you need, and watch all the ways in which He helps you.

Nothing is impossible for God—and it's to that height we should pray to. "If you have faith when you pray, you will be given whatever you ask for" (Matthew 21:22 CEV).

Prayers

✳ *Heavenly Father, help me to believe more and more each day in all that You can do. Help me to be as a child—Your child—and to simply believe all that You're telling me.*

✳ *Lord Jesus, increase my faith. Give me a faith that's so full it spills out onto those around me. Help my life to be a lamp through which You show what faith looks like.*

✳ *Holy Spirit, pour into me a greater degree of believing, so that nothing before me seems impossible—so I more fully know that with God, nothing is impossible.*

Spiritual Growth

✳ **Influence the world:** Set your heart on becoming a soul through which God can shine His light of hope into the darkened world around you. Though you may be surrounded by unbelievers—or believers who just don't believe very much—be that one in a thousand who influences the world around them with the God within them. *Our faith can be so full that it spills over onto those around us.* Jesus promised us, "You shall receive power when the Holy Spirit has come upon you; and you shall be witnesses to Me in Jerusalem, and in all Judea and Samaria, and to the end of the earth" (Acts 1:8).

✳ **Minister to others:** Be ready at any given moment to speak a word for the Lord to the person standing before you. God places people before us and wants us to be His vessel to them. You don't have to preach a sermon, but only give an encouraging word. *Stop criticizing people for what they're not, and start encouraging people for what they could be. People are hungry for someone to simply believe in them. Be the blessing. Be the encourager. Be to others what you pray* *others would be to you.* Seek to "comfort the fainthearted, uphold the weak, be patient with all" (1 Thessalonians 5:14).

- **Believe all things are possible:** Decide in your heart today that you'll believe God can do anything. Pray this truth back to God. Write it down and proclaim it over your life and the lives around you. Write down verses from the Word of God that proclaim this truth and place them where you spend your time. Child of God, you can believe. *Believe like a believer.* "Jesus said to him, 'If you can believe, all things are possible to him who believes'" (Mark 9:23).

Acknowledgments

Mary Balius, my best friend and precious wife. Your sweet nature and gentle spirit make for a blessed home from where I can write. You are my most treasured gift from the Lord.

My parents, Herbert and Patricia Balius, who have been my model for godly living and the greatest intercessors for my ministry.

My children and grandchildren, who are such a blessing to me and inspire me to be better than I am.

Thomas Womack, who has blessed me with his masterful work in editing this book. http://www.bookox.com/

Tamara Dever from TLC Book Design, I am eternally grateful for your patience and your guidance. https://tlcbookdesign.com/

Monica Thomas from TLC Book Design, whose mastery of cover and interior designing is inspiring.

Dana Cobb, also from TLC Book Design, whose precision with proofreading is incredible.

I want to thank the many precious souls who have poured into my life and blessed me with their friendship, counsel, and prayers. I could never name everyone here, but your names are written on my heart and spoken in my prayers.

About the Author

Paul Balius is an author and teacher, devoted to helping God's children grow in their faith. Paul spent fourteen years in prison ministry, the last seven teaching and preaching in several prisons. The Lord called Paul out of the prisons and into solitude where he could begin writing for the kingdom.

Paul has written thousands of devotions and hundreds of blogs. He is publishing books in the hope to reach even one. His passion is to help people to unlock the mystery of the power of God into their life. Paul believes there is nothing impossible for God, not even you.

Paul and his wife Mary currently reside in Orange, California.

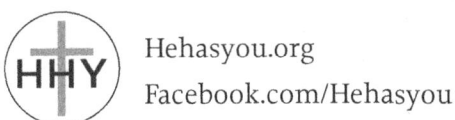

Hehasyou.org
Facebook.com/Hehasyou

Do you sense that you were meant for something more?

You were meant for something more, and the something more is nothing less than being filled with the Spirit of God.

Do you long to walk in a higher faith with a deeper sense of the presence of the Holy Spirit?

Do you long to hear the voice of the Lord speaking into your life?

Do you long to have spiritual gifts that you might serve God with them?

6 x 9" paperback, 204 pages
Also available in ebook

In *The Promise of the Holy Spirit*, you will learn:

- About the promises of God for you.
- Coming to know the Holy Spirit.
- Being filled with the Holy Spirit.
- Being changed by the Holy Spirit.
- How to hear the Holy Spirit.
- Being led by the Holy Spirit.
- How to receive prophetic words.
- Discovering your spiritual gifts.
- How to reach a higher faith.

Are you ready to go to the next level in your faith? Get your copy of *The Promise of the Holy Spirit* and take hold of all that God has in store for you.

Made in the USA
Las Vegas, NV
20 December 2023

83268423R00125